The Power of a
PRAYING®
Grandparent

STORMIE
OMARTIAN

HARVEST HOUSE PUBLISHERS
EUGENE, OREGON

Cover by Nicole Dougherty

Back cover author photo © Michael Gomez Photography

THE POWER OF A PRAYING is a registered trademark of The Hawkins Children's LLC. Harvest House Publishers, Inc., is the exclusive licensee of the federally registered trademark THE POWER OF A PRAYING.

THE POWER OF A PRAYING® GRANDPARENT
Copyright © 2016 by Stormie Omartian
Published by Harvest House Publishers
Eugene, Oregon 97408
www.harvesthousepublishers.com

ISBN 978-0-7369-6300-8 (pbk.)
ISBN 978-0-7369-6301-5 (eBook)

Library of Congress Cataloging-in-Publication Data
Names: Omartian, Stormie, author.
Title: The power of a praying grandparent / Stormie Omartian.
Description: Eugene, Oregon : Harvest House Publishers, 2016.
Identifiers: LCCN 2016016701 (print) | LCCN 2016017735 (ebook) | ISBN 9780736963008 (pbk.) | ISBN 9780736963015 ()
Subjects: LCSH: Grandparents—Religious life. | Grandparents—Prayers and devotions. | Intercessory prayer—Christianity.
Classification: LCC BV4528.5 .O43 2016 (print) | LCC BV4528.5 (ebook) | DDC 248.3/20853—dc23
LC record available at https://lccn.loc.gov/2016016701

Printed in the United States of America

23 24 / BP-JC / 13

The mercy of the LORD is from
everlasting to everlasting
on those who fear Him,
and His righteousness to children's children,
to such as keep His covenant,
and to those who remember
His commandments to do them.

PSALM 103:17-18

Contents

SECTION TWO
Praying for Your Grandchildren's Safety and Protection

SECTION THREE
Praying for Your Grandchildren's Spiritual Growth and Development

Section Four
Praying for Your Grandchildren's Provision and Well-Being

The Lifelong Gift of a Praying Grandparent

An amazing thing happens in your heart when you see your grandchild for the first time. It's difficult to explain. Though it's different from having your own children, the experience is what every grandparent has told you for years that it would be. Nothing else is quite like it. There is an instant and deep connection. There is unconditional love that is unimaginable before that moment. It is profoundly special. Uniquely moving. And irrevocably life altering.

This doesn't minimize the unconditional love we felt for our own children or the moving and life-altering experience we have when they come into our life. But, as grandparents, we don't have the major physical and emotional journey of getting our grandchildren here. They are gifts that are laid in our laps— often literally. That's not to say we aren't constantly prayerful and concerned for the safety and health of our daughter or daughter-in-law—the one who carries her precious cargo to what we pray is perfect development. We also pray for our son or son-in-law to be a good support for his wife, an excellent provider, and a great father for his children—which can seem quite overwhelming to most new fathers who are in touch with the reality of all that.

I remember when Michael and I first became parents. The process engulfed us. Whether it was self-doubt about our ability to be good parents, or we feared what could happen to our child, or we felt unprepared, the process was our focus. No matter how many books I read on child rearing or classes I took on what to do after our child was born, the journey consumed me. And that is true for most people—whether the child was theirs biologically, or by adoption, or through marriage. The road to the child's arrival could seem scary, and there were no guarantees.

Our grown children may have many of those same fears too.

Besides all this, the process of bringing forth and raising children is exhausting. The sleep factor—or lack thereof—complicates things when parents are trying not to neglect their spouse and marriage. This can seem like an overwhelming task. If one spouse is not even in the picture—for whatever reason—and the parent raising the child is a single mom or dad, the worry factor goes up greatly. A single mom or dad may be the only one in charge of the rent, mortgage, food, clothing, medical care, schooling, and every other need of the child or children. Without having the emotional support of someone to share the duties of being a good parent, the responsibility can seem impossible.

As grandparents, we usually don't fully carry the same burdens the way a parent does, although these things concern us greatly. That is, unless the child is not only laid in our lap, but also the total responsibility for our grandchild is laid entirely on our shoulders because the parent or parents cannot care for their daughter or son. Many grandparents experience that.

Whatever your situation, consider yourself blessed to have a precious grandchild. So many people are grieved because they will never have one, or the one they had is no longer in their lives. Thank God every day that you have the privilege and the power in prayer of affecting your grandchildren's lives in ways you may not even imagine.

The Gift of a Praying "Gramma" or "Grampa"

Grandchildren are a gift from God to you. And your prayers are a gift to them that can touch them for a lifetime—even after you are no longer around to see all of the good results. God has an important ministry for you to your grandchild or grandchildren—not only in word and deed, but also in prayer.

Personally, I didn't have a praying mother or father—at least, not to my knowledge. But I did have one praying grandmother. I didn't realize this for years because I only saw her twice in my life—once when I was about six, and another time when I was around twelve. She was my father's mother, and she seemed to be a kind, gentle, and caring person.

It was later in my life, after I was married and had two children of my own, that my severely mentally ill mother died of cancer at the age of 64, and we asked my dad to come live with us. He was in his mid-seventies at the time, and we gave him an entire wing of our house that allowed him three rooms to himself plus a small parlor, all at the front of the house where he could have privacy and yet be with the rest of the family whenever he wanted. Every day he sat in the parlor watching for the children to come home from school. They were in grade school and high school during that time, and they loved to sit with him and hear him tell stories about his life. He'd had so many near-death experiences, such as being struck by lightning *twice*, hit by a train, shot with a gun, falling into a ravine on horseback, and losing control of his truck on an icy mountain road and going over the side of the mountain—just to name a few. It was amazing to think that he lived to be 93 and died quietly in his own bed as he slept.

I, too, had escaped death so many times in my life—including pneumonia when I was a baby and diphtheria when I was about six, for starters. There would be more perilous instances to come. After I received the Lord at 28 and walked with Him for two decades, I saw that my heavenly Father had His hand on me all along. One day in prayer, I asked God who had been praying for me because I realized at that point someone must have been. And I could think of no one on my mother's side. Her mother—my maternal grandmother—died in childbirth when my mother was 11. And my own mother was too mentally ill all of my life.

I asked my father about *his* mother, and I discovered that she was a faithful, godly woman of prayer. So faithful to God was she that every Sunday morning she walked with her children a very long way—even in freezing snow—across fields and down country roads to church. There was no such thing as children's church there, so my father sat on hard wooden pews for four hours in the morning, four more hours in the evening, and then again on Wednesday night as well. He said that his father never went to church, nor did he *take* them to church. So once my dad became an adult, he swore he would never enter a church again. And except for a funeral and a wedding, as far as I know he never did.

In answer to my prayer, God showed me that it was my father's mother who prayed for her eight children and her many grandchildren, and that was the reason my dad and I escaped death so many times. Even though she died when I was only a teenager, I feel it was her prayers that continued to cover me in my life.

My dad was always a good grandfather to my children. He never prayed that I know of, but when I asked him openly if he believed in God and that Jesus was the Son of God who died for us and rose again to give us eternal life with Him—because I wanted to be certain I would see my dad in heaven one day—he said emphatically, "Yes, of course!" as if to say, "Who in their right mind wouldn't believe that?"

That was good enough for me.

While he lived with us, he taught my daughter how to plant and grow a garden in our backyard, and they tended it every day. He taught my son how to play many games, and they played them every chance they got. Michael and I didn't have time for some of the things he could do. He was the only grandparent my children ever knew well because their grandmothers both died of breast cancer, and my husband's father lived far away and also died when they were young. But they were able to spend time with my father every day, and he and my children experienced a mutual and special love for one another.

A godly grandmother or grandfather is always welcome in a child's life. But being a godly *praying* "Gramma" or "Grampa" is a gift you can deliberately give your grandchildren even if you don't see them often. And if you don't have a grandchild in your life *yet*, ask God to show you who needs a spiritual "Gramma" or "Grampa." There are so many who do.

I have had the joy of being a part of my grandchildren's lives from the time they were born. And even before that—while they were growing in their mother's womb—I prayed countless times daily for them to be healthy and perfectly formed. In fact, I was praying for my grandchildren even before my own children were married—well before I knew I would even have any.

You may have become a grandparent because one of your children married someone who already had a child. And that child may already have two sets of grandparents in their life. But you may not know whether the grandparents are praying. No matter what the circumstances are, your prayers are still a needed gift for that child.

A grandchild can never have too much prayer or too much love.

Not long after my book *The Power of a Praying Parent* came out in 1995 and had sold a few million copies, many people were asking me, "When are you going to write *The Power of a Praying Grandparent?*" I told them that while I was certainly old enough to be a grandmother, my children weren't doing *their* part. I was still praying about them finding the right person to marry, and I didn't want to write about something I had never personally experienced. I chose to wait until I had the joy of being a grandmother before I wrote this book. Now that I have two precious grandchildren, I feel at liberty to write it.

This book is divided into *four important sections*—or areas of prayer—to help you easily find the prayer topic you want.

The first prayer in each section will be for you to pray for yourself as a grandparent. It will help you to understand how vitally important and long lasting your prayers are for each of your grandchildren. Even if you don't see them often, your role in their lives is more far-reaching than you may realize.

The second prayer in each section will be for the parents of each grandchild. They face serious challenges coming at them from all angles, and they desperately need your covering in prayer whether they realize it or not. In fact, one of the best ways you can pray for your grandchildren is to ask God to help their parents or stepparents to raise them well.

Following those first two prayers in each section will be five prayers for your grandchild or grandchildren. It doesn't matter if your grandchildren are small, teenagers, or adults. I guarantee they need your prayers.

I encourage you to not only pray alone as often as you can, but whenever possible, pray with others as well. There is power in praying together with one or two people about anything that concerns you. Jesus said, "*If two of you agree* on earth concerning anything that they ask, *it will be done for them* by My Father in heaven. For where two or three are gathered together in My name, *I am there in the midst of them*" (Matthew 18:19-20). The powerful promise of God's presence when we pray with others is too great a gift to ignore.

I added the italics in these verses above, and I have added them in other Scriptures throughout the book as well. So that I won't have to keep repeating the words "emphasis added," just know that when you see italics in Scripture, I have added them to bring special notice to certain words.

You can start praying from chapter 1 through to the end of chapter 28. Each chapter is short and includes a prayer and a page of Scriptures to back it up. Or you can pick and choose which section and chapter you feel is the most-needed area of prayer focus at that time for your grandchild.

Oh, and please do not take offense at my frequent use of the word "grandchildren" if you have one grandchild. It's just that the plural word keeps me from having to frequently use the words "he or she." Believe me, one precious grandchild is more than enough for you to have plenty to pray about.

Praying for Your Grandchildren's Understanding of Godly Love and Relationships

1

Lord, Enable Me to Clearly Express Love for Each of My Grandchildren

*E*very child is unique. Each child—even in the same family—is different from the others in that family. We can't think that every grandchild has the same strengths, thoughts, or needs. Nor can we assume that he or she experiences the same events in the exact way the other family members do. Dynamics in a family change all the time. And so do the perceptions of a child.

That being said, every child has the same basic needs. Next to being fed, clothed, and housed with care, the greatest need of each child is for love. But even then, every child perceives and receives love differently. What we as grandparents must learn is the best way for us to express *our* love for each child.

Ask God to help you communicate love to each of your grand-children in a way he or she can clearly understand and receive. Only He knows for sure what is in the heart of a child.

Some people have trouble communicating love—even for their own children or grandchildren. It's not that they don't love them. In fact, they probably love them deeply. It's just that they cannot express it well. Often, that particular person was raised in a similar way themselves. Love was withheld or not communicated well enough to them, so they didn't believe that they were loved.

That was my own experience. I don't ever recall either of my parents saying "I love you" to me. Nor did I ever hear it from any of my extended family members either—not that they should have said anything because I was isolated from them for the most part. My mother acted as though she hated me. She was physically and verbally abusive, and she locked me in a closet for much of my early childhood. But she was mentally ill, and her illness became more apparent as the years went on.

My dad was never abusive. He was kind but not affectionate. He later told me, after I was an adult, that he and my mother had decided to never communicate anything good or encouraging to me about myself so that I would never be spoiled. I remember thinking, *What a terrible idea!* And I vowed to never do that to my own children. I was going to make sure they knew they were loved—by God and me—and I asked God to help me do it well.

I realized early on that I was too damaged to know how to receive love from another person, and I didn't know how to reciprocate it, either. It wasn't until I received the love of God that I was able to truly give and receive love.

The person I loved most growing up was my baby sister, who was born when I was 12. She was the best thing that ever happened to our family and to me. I basically raised her because my mother told me that when I wasn't in school, she was mine. But that didn't bother me much because I was crazy about her. However, after I was out of high school, I had to leave home to

escape all the verbal abuse from my mother and the strife it created in the family. I always felt guilt for abandoning my sister,
but I knew I had to get out of that toxic environment in order
to help my sister get out one day as well. Besides, I believed that
with me gone, the house would be more peaceful.

Apparently I was wrong about that.

While my mother was never cruel to my sister the way she
was to me, I later learned how much my sister was neglected
and in many ways felt abandoned. I didn't realize how badly
until I heard about it in her own words. I felt terrible about all
that had happened to her, but I didn't know what else I *could*
have done at that time.

We were two sisters from the same family who had different experiences and perceptions. It was a shock to me when I
offered to send my sister to college or open up a shop for her
to display her artwork, which was professional quality, that she
didn't want either option. I had always determined to get as far
away as I could from the way I had grown up. She, on the other
hand, felt hopeless and didn't have the self-confidence to even
want to do any of that. I eventually accepted the fact that all the
things *I* wanted for her were not what she wanted for herself.

In some families, children feel they are not as loved as their
siblings. People have shared that kind of experience with me
so many times, and although it's quite possible that this is
true, it could also be that this is their own perception of family dynamics because love wasn't communicated in a way they
could clearly perceive. Real or not, it still leaves a scar.

One of the Greatest Gifts of Love

*One of the greatest gifts of love you can give to your grandchil-
dren are your prayers for them.*

Among the many rewards of prayer, one of the most amazing is that not only do you grow to love the person you pray for, but as you pray for that person, they seem to sense your love—or the love of God—through your prayers. When people say, "I felt your prayers," that is what they are sensing even if they don't understand what it is. The reason for that is as you draw close to God in prayer for someone, God's love is deepened in your own heart. So the more time you spend talking to God, the more His love is poured *into you,* and the more it overflows *through you.*

God is love, and as you pray you are in contact with all that He is. When you pray for another person, you receive God's heart of love for him or her.

Another amazing thing that happens is that as you pray for someone, God can soften that person's heart toward *you.* There is a transference of God's love to the person for whom you are praying. I cannot prove that it always happens, but I have experienced it enough times—and so have countless others—that it cannot be denied.

I had an extended family member who was very rude and unaccepting of me for a reason I couldn't understand. I hardly knew him. But after I received the Lord and learned about the power of prayer in Jesus' name, I started praying for him to open his heart to the love of God. Amazingly, my heart softened toward him. But not only that, when I saw him again years later, he greeted me like a long-lost friend. I saw no reason for him to reject me in the first place, nor did I know of anything that happened to cause him to suddenly accept me. It had to be because of the prayers. The only contact I had with him in those years were those two times. But I have experienced this kind of thing many times, so there is a powerful dynamic that happens when praying for people to open their heart to the love of God.

Even if you live far from your grandchildren and don't see them often, your calls, cards, letters, emails, videos, and thoughtful gifts can have a major impact on their life—especially if you often tell them you are always praying to God for them. Ask them to tell you any specific needs they want you to pray about for them. Your prayers can help establish a bond of love between you and your grandchildren—even from a distance.

Removing the Barriers

Jesus taught us how to take authority in the spirit realm in order to effect change in the physical realm. He said, "*Have faith in God.* For assuredly, I say to you, *whoever says to this mountain, 'Be removed and be cast into the sea,' and does not doubt in his heart,* but believes that those things he says will be done, *he will have whatever he says.* Therefore I say to you, *whatever things you ask when you pray, believe that you receive them, and you will have them*" (Mark 11:22-24).

This is a great Scripture to apply to any family member where there may exist a mountain of resistance to expressing or receiving love. That kind of barrier can seem as impossible to move as a real mountain. Yet Jesus said it could be done if we have faith in *His power* and *His will* to do it. Helping people to love others—and *receive* love from others—is always God's will. But there can be an invisible wall that keeps someone from *receiving* love or a mountainlike barrier rendering them incapable of *communicating* love. In either case, it can cause something akin to emotional paralysis in a family unless this mountain is first reduced to ashes in prayer.

Ask God to reveal if you have any barriers to giving or receiving love. This is very important. If you have felt unloved in your past, it could affect how you show love to your children and grandchildren today. Or if there is unforgiveness in your heart of any kind, this can put up major barriers, and people can sense them without knowing exactly what they are. God says He won't listen to our prayers until we confess anything in our heart that should not be there. (See Psalm 66:18.)

We can be hurt by the things our children or their spouses say or do. But we have to let it go and get completely free of it because if we don't, it will affect our heart, our relationships, and our close walk with the Lord. Ask God if you have any hurt in your heart that needs to be brought to Him so He can heal the hurt and break down every barrier creeping in to become a stronghold of division.

Family relationships can be very delicate—especially where in-laws are concerned. Pray that God will enable you to always walk a line of love, graciousness, kindness, mercy, wisdom, generosity, and forgiveness. Ask Him to break down any barrier to love flowing from you to your children, grandchildren, or other family members—including in-laws.

Only God knows what will communicate our love and His to our family members. The thing is, people sense unforgiveness in our hearts even if it is not directed toward them, and even if they don't know what it is they are sensing. We owe it to our grandchildren to get rid of it so our hearts are clean before the Lord and our prayers are effective.

We all need a heart that is filled with unconditional love for our children and grandchildren, and the ability to communicate it clearly—unhindered and unfiltered. Let's pray for that.

My Prayer to God

Lord, I lift up my grandchildren to You. (Name each grandchild before God.) Show me how to express my deep, unconditional love for each of them in a way they can clearly perceive and receive. Reveal to me the many ways I can demonstrate my love for each child.

I pray that You will remove any barriers in me that have been formed through disappointment or pain in my past. If there is a place in my heart where I feel rejected or unloved, I bring that to You for healing. If there is any unforgiveness in me toward anyone, show me and I will confess it. I know Your Word says if I keep that kind of sin in my heart, You will not listen to my prayers until I have cleared the slate with You (Psalm 66:18). I don't want to carry anything in my heart that shouldn't be there. Set me completely free from all unforgiveness today so there is no mountain of separation between me and my children or grandchildren. Keep my heart clean so that my prayers are never hindered.

If there are any other strongholds of separation or breaches of relationships in my family, dissolve those completely. Burn away any barriers to total forgiveness in the hearts of the people involved. Help me to pray so powerfully for my grandchildren that they sense Your love and mine for them. Enable my prayers to touch them deeply and create a bond of love between us.

Enable me to be one of the "peacemakers" You have described in Your Word. I know that functioning in that role distinguishes me as a child of Yours (Matthew 5:9). I pray for Your peace that passes all understanding to reign in my family—and the families of my children and grandchildren.

In Jesus' name I pray.

God's Word to Me

If I regard iniquity in my heart,
the Lord will not hear.

PSALM 66:18

The discretion of a man makes him slow to anger,
and his glory is to overlook a transgression.

PROVERBS 19:11

Judge not, and you shall not be judged.
Condemn not, and you shall not be condemned.
Forgive, and you will be forgiven.

LUKE 6:37

The spirit of a man is the lamp of the LORD,
searching all the inner depths of his heart.

PROVERBS 20:27

Whatever you ask the Father in My name
He will give you…
Ask, and you will receive, that your joy may be full.

JOHN 16:23-24

2

Lord, Grow Love in My Grandchildren's Parents for Their Children and Each Other

Not only are grandchildren one of the greatest gifts we can have on this earth, watching our children become good parents is a wonderful experience as well. The reward for any parent who has spent a lifetime working, supporting, and raising his or her children is to eventually see them choose a good husband or wife and become great parents. But our children need a lot of prayer support in order to walk successfully through all of the seasons of life.

I am blessed to have a wonderful daughter-in-law who is a great wife and gifted mother. She is generous in letting me take care of my granddaughters a couple days a week. I find those times some of the most rewarding of my life—although definitely exhausting! But for me it's almost like a vacation from my daily work of writing and traveling and all the other things I do to run a home, business, and ministry. I consider caring for them my highest reward—right up next to having a marriage that has lasted more than 43 years and enjoying good health on most days.

It's also a great reward to see my son be such a good father to his little girls and so helpful to his wife. He and his wife are truly a team, and they are raising children who are happy, healthy, affectionate, good tempered, godly, and well behaved. I thank God every day for all that and do not take these great blessings lightly. I fully realize that not everyone has this, but I also know that I was praying for this very thing from the time my own children were born. If you have not been praying about these things for that long, don't worry. Your fervent prayers now can make up for lost time.

That's why I believe it's good to not only pray for yourself to be the best grandparent you can be—even from afar if you have to—but also to pray for the parents of your grandchildren to be the best and most loving parents for their children.

Pray first of all that the parents will love their children the way God wants them to—that is, always with their best interests at heart. Along with that, pray that the parents of your grandchildren will grow in love for each other. This is crucial. The more solid, happy, and loving their relationship is, the more stable, secure, and loved the children will feel about themselves and their lives. This is true even if the parents are divorced, or one or the other is no longer in the picture for whatever reason.

Pray that there will be *love* and *respect* between each parent, especially where their children are concerned. No matter what the situation, pray that there will be *peace* and *unity* between the parents, and that they will come to an *agreement* about how their children are to be raised.

Always pray that there will be no divorce in their future.

Even if divorce has already happened—or seems inevitable—
pray for the best possible situation. Ask God to help the parents put their children first and not perpetuate strife between
each other. Pray especially that the parents will never bring
their children into their fight, but instead will invite the love
of God to flow between them.

If either a mother or a father of your grandchildren has
already remarried, pray for the new stepmother or stepfather
to be a godly, loving, supportive stepparent to your grandchildren. He or she very much needs your prayers as well because
of this new relationship he or she has with your grandchildren.

The best position for you to take is not to judge any one
of them. There is plenty of judgment to go around already.
Besides, they don't need judgment; they need forgiveness. And
they need the love of God in a big way. Your top concern is for
your grandchildren, who greatly need to know that they are
loved—by God, by you, by each of their parents, and also by
their stepparents.

It's complicated, I know.

*But God's love is not complicated. It is simply without lim-
its, and it is unfailing. Your grandchildren need to know they can
depend on His love, and so do their parents.*

When children witness the love of God in their parents—
even divorced parents—and see a godly respect and love for
one another, it's easier for them to receive the love of God
themselves. We've all seen disasters happen to children of
divorce as too many walk away from God, carry unforgiveness in their heart for one or both parents, have trouble trusting others and forming relationships that last, and much more.
The Scripture that says, *"Above all things have fervent love for
one another, for 'love will cover a multitude of sins'"* is especially

applicable here (1 Peter 4:8). The couple who divorce but can still express love for each other and their children will have the greatest success with how their children go through life.

Pray that your grandchildren's parents will be filled with the love of God so they can communicate His love to their children in a way they can clearly perceive. A life filled with the love of God and the love of family is a life of peace. And we want all that for our grandchildren in the biggest way.

Being a Consistent Part of Your Grandchildren's Lives

Pray that your grandchildren's parents will love them enough to always let you be a part of their lives. Pray also that all of your children's grandparents will love their grandchildren enough to maintain a loving heart toward both of the parents. Pray that the parents never use the grandchildren to punish the grandparents, which I have seen happen way too often.

I know of a mom and dad who are strong believers and grandparents to several little ones in one of their children's family, but they are not allowed to see their grandchildren at all. This is not because they are bad people or are a threat to their grandchildren. They are wonderful, godly people who serve God full-time. Their child parted ways because of a business disagreement and has totally cut them off from seeing his family. The grandparents were a big part of their grandchildren's lives from birth until this happened, but for the past five years all ties have been severed. They have been completely shut out. They can't communicate with their grandchildren in any way—not even on birthdays or holidays—all because of differences of opinion about money. The suffering these grandparents have endured is cruel and heartbreaking, not to mention what sadness and confusion their grandchildren must be experiencing.

I realize in some cases that parents may feel there is a danger for their children due to the infirmity or forgetfulness of the grandparent, or a grandparent is into things that are not good for children to be around. But even so, the children could still be brought for a visit on a birthday. Or the grandparents could meet the parents and children someplace. Of course, if there is any sort of abuse on a grandparent's part, that negates everything. But this situation I described was more an act of revenge—a punishment of the grandparents because of a family business matter. Unfortunately, it punishes the grandchildren as well.

This kind of barrier to the flow of God's love causes grandchildren to lose so much. Grandparents are something we don't have with us forever. They are a priceless gift. Not everyone has them, but everyone needs at least one in his or her life. Pray for the breaking down of any mountain of hardheartedness or revenge when you see it—especially when the needs of grandchildren are not taken into consideration.

Another thing to pray about is that the grandparents never use the grandchildren to punish the parents. I know this may seem odd, but it is not as uncommon as you might think.

I know of parents who did not approve of the young woman their son married, so they did not go to their wedding and have never seen their three grandchildren, the oldest of whom is now ten. It's difficult to imagine hearts so hard. I have known the young wife since she was born, and there is no justification for this behavior. These grandparents are not only missing out on the greatest blessings of having these three beautiful grandchildren in their lives—the only ones they have—but they are also depriving their grandchildren of what could be a great blessing by not ever seeing them or expressing their love for them.

These are all believers in Christ I am talking about! They are always in church—worshipping God—but still refusing to forgive their son for not marrying the girl of *their* choice. And not forgiving the daughter-in-law for "ruining their son's life." If this is a story of believers, I can only imagine how often this occurs with unbelievers who do *not* have the "love of Christ" flowing in their lives. Fortunately, I also know the grandparents on the wife's side, and they are exactly the opposite. They constantly show their deep and unconditional love for these three precious children and are very active in their lives.

I hate to even bring this up, but in certain cases, it may be necessary to pray—for your grandchildren's sake—that God will help you love your son-in-law or daughter-in-law the way He wants you to. I am blessed to not have a problem with this because both my daughter-in-law and my son-in-law are wonderful, godly people. I love them both very much and thank God for them every day. But I know countless people who *do* have this problem, and perhaps for a good reason. Even so, this has to change. It's not God's will to resent or be unloving toward a daughter-in-law or son-in-law. It grieves the Holy Spirit in us. If that is the situation for you, ask God to put love in your heart for that person, and then pray for him or her to have the love of God in their heart for you. We grow to love the person we pray for, even though we may not love what they do or who they are at that moment. We can love them as God's child whom He wants to save, deliver, and grow into His likeness. This is extremely important.

Pray that all the grandparents in your family love all the parents of their grandchildren.

Love covers all and heals all. And it pleases God.

My Prayer to God

Lord, I lift up to You my grandchildren's parents. (<u>Name each parent before God.</u>) Help them to get along as a couple and not allow strife or arguments to pull them apart. Teach them to seek harmony, unity, and peace in their home every day. I pray they will love each other and not allow a spirit of divorce to break up their family. I know my prayers will not stop a selfish or strong-willed person from doing what he or she is intent on doing, but I know You hear my prayers and can enable a person to better hear from You—if he or she desires to do so.

I pray that each parent of my grandchildren will be able to express his or her love for his or her children in ways that can be clearly perceived so that the children always feel loved. Fill the parents with Your love so that it overflows from them to their children. Give them obvious signs of love—such as mercy, forgiveness, patience, generosity of heart, acceptance, and encouragement—not only for their children, but also for one another. Remind them to make their children a priority, next to their love for You and each other. Give them the ability to communicate their love to their children in a way that makes it clear to them.

Where divorce has already occurred between parents, I pray for a softening of hearts so that a godly love can be seen between the parents toward each other as well as for the children. Keep them from ever sacrificing their children on the altar of workaholism or selfish pursuits. I pray that the parents will never use their children to punish each other or the grandparents because of a spirit of revenge, which is totally against Your will. Help them to put their children's needs first before themselves. Only You can work all that in the hearts of everyone concerned.

In Jesus' name I pray.

God's Word to Me

If God so loved us, we also ought to love one another.
No one has seen God at any time. If we love one another,
God abides in us, and His love has been perfected in us.

1 John 4:11-12

Beloved, let us love one another, for love is of God;
and everyone who loves is born of God and knows God.

1 John 4:7

Though I speak with the tongues of men and of angels,
but have not love,
I have become sounding brass or a clanging cymbal.

1 Corinthians 13:1

Bear one another's burdens,
and so fulfill the law of Christ.

Galatians 6:2

Though I have the gift of prophecy,
and understand all mysteries and all knowledge,
and though I have all faith,
so that I could remove mountains,
but have not love, I am nothing.

1 Corinthians 13:2

3

Lord, Help My Grandchildren Understand How Much You Love Them

oo many people have grown to adulthood, even to old age, never knowing or understanding how much they are loved by God. And the result is often unrest in their soul, grief in their heart, and many problems in their life. We don't want that for our grandchildren. Or our children. Or us.

The earlier your grandchildren learn how much God loves them, the better their lives will be. The more they know about who Jesus is, and what He has done, the more they will understand the depth of His love for them. The more time they spend with Him—talking to Him in prayer and listening to Him speak to their heart—the happier they will be.

Jesus said that the kingdom of God can only be found, or experienced, by people who come to Him with a heart like a little child's.

When the people around Jesus were bringing their children to Him so He could touch them, the disciples rebuked them because they thought children were not important enough to take up His time. When Jesus saw what was happening, He was displeased and said, "*Let the little children come to Me, and do not forbid them; for of such is the kingdom of God*" (Mark 10:14). He went on to explain, saying, "*Whoever does not receive the kingdom of God as a little child will by no means enter it*" (verse 15). Then He picked them up and blessed them.

Jesus loves little children—especially their humility and purity of heart.

It took me a long time to realize how much God loves me. I felt unloved my whole life, even years after I received the Lord. I felt God's love in the church I attended. It was palpable there. I saw it in the believing people and in the pastors—the people in whom the Holy Spirit of God dwelled. The Bible says, "You are not in the flesh but in the Spirit, if indeed the Spirit of God dwells in you. *Now if anyone does not have the Spirit of Christ, he is not His*" (Romans 8:9). That means when we receive Jesus, we have His Spirit of love, peace, and joy residing in our hearts. That is the first step to receiving the love of God. But why does it take some of us so long to really believe it?

After I received the Lord, I knew God loved other people. I just didn't believe He loved me. I know this is a quick and abbreviated explanation of why I felt that way, but it had to do with my own unforgiveness toward my father for never rescuing me from my mother's abuse. A Christian counselor who had previously led me through great deliverance brought it up to me and explained what God had revealed to her. I came to realize that when the people who are supposed to love you don't—or you *feel* they don't—it erects a barrier in your heart that prevents you from fully believing *anyone* loves you, even God. It makes love difficult to trust.

If there is unforgiveness—not only toward the abuser, but

also toward the one who didn't put a stop to the abuse—it keeps you from receiving complete restoration. It stops up your life so you cannot fully receive God's love because you can't trust Him enough to receive all He has for you. Once I recognized that unforgiveness in my heart and I confessed it to the Lord, I forgave my father. (I had already forgiven my mother.) It was then I began to truly sense God's love for me. And it has grown every year since then.

Explaining God's Love to Your Grandchildren

Children first see the love of God in their parents. But if a parent communicates all judgment and no mercy, the child grows up seeing only the negative things about himself or herself. That is, unless someone reinforces how much they are loved—by God, by parents, by grandparents, and by other family members. In situations where the deep, unfailing, unconditional love of God is missing from the heart of a mother or father, it could be that you are the one in your grandchild's life who can manifest this wonderful love of God toward them.

Ask God to help you explain to your grandchildren—in an age-appropriate way—how much God loves them and wants them to talk to Him in their prayers. You can tell them that God is always with them, and that He wants to guide them and help them do what's right. You can assure them that He wants to provide what they need and to protect them.

Because it is never too soon to teach a child to pray, the sooner we can teach our grandchildren to talk to God, the sooner they will get to know Him and understand His love for them.

My husband and I taught our children early to fold their hands and say thank you to God for their food, and pray for God to help them during the day, and to protect them at night when they went to sleep. They learned to thank Him for everything and to pray for other people who needed His help. They never knew life without praying.

We have watched our son and daughter-in-law teaching their children to pray from the time they were about a year old. We love to see those little folded hands as they thank God for their food or pray before they go to sleep. We try to reinforce everything their parents are doing whenever our grandchildren come to spend the night with us.

I want to emphasize that, just as it is never too early to teach a child to pray, it is never too late to teach a child to pray, either.

Even if your grandchildren are older or grown up, and to your knowledge do not pray, you can still ask them if you can pray *for* them. Or perhaps *with* them. It may seem hard to initiate that if they are older or in adulthood, but you can ask them if they have a need or concern they want you to pray about for them. I have found that most people—even unbelievers—still want prayer. And especially from a grandparent they know loves them.

The peace we want our grandchildren to know is the kind that comes only from God. It's beyond human understanding. It's the peace that is found in the midst of problems, pain, chaos, and turmoil—the kind that makes no sense in light of what is happening. We have the peace that passes all understanding because of God's Spirit of love and peace within us.

It brings us great peace to know how much God loves us—a peace that is not possible without Him.

I have a book at my house that plays "Jesus Loves Me" sung

by little children. When my two-year-old granddaughter comes into my house, she runs to that book and pushes the button so the song can play while she looks at the illustrations showing the ways Jesus shows His love for us. Then she pushes the button again so she can sing and dance along with it. Out of the mouth of babes comes perfect praise. She plays it over and over, and I guarantee that when she leaves my house that song is still playing in her mind and heart. I know it certainly is in mine.

Whenever you get a chance, talk to your grandchildren about all the things that are good about their lives and how all good things come from God because He loves them. Tell them how love is like the wind and you can't see it, but you can *feel* it. Point out the countless ways that God shows His love to them. Show them how He has given them a family, a home, food, sun, rain, and protection, and point out all of the other many ways He provides for them. Tell them about the promises of God in the Bible and how God keeps His promises because He loves them. Assure them that nothing can ever separate them from God's love. Even when they do something wrong, God never stops loving them. He just asks them to come to Him and say, "Lord, I'm sorry and I don't want to ever do it again." And He promises to forgive them and not allow anything to separate them from His love.

Most of all, pray that God will pour out His Spirit of love on your grandchildren and upon their parents as well so that they will live in the peace that only His love can bring.

Our lives are always happier when we feel and trust God's love for us.

My Prayer to God

Lord, I pray that You will pour out Your love on my grandchildren. (Name each grandchild before God.) I know they can never be truly at peace in themselves until they are at peace with You. I pray that my grandchildren will know You well and have hearts that are filled with Your love, peace, and joy so they will live peaceful lives. Help them "to know the love of Christ which passes knowledge" so that they will experience the fullness of all that You are, and all that You have for them (Ephesians 3:19). Open their hearts to trust that nothing can separate them from Your love—not even their own mistakes. That's because when they say they are sorry to You and promise to not do it again, You forgive them. Teach them that You love us all enough to correct us when we get off the path You have for us.

Help me teach my grandchildren that when we look to You first, You provide everything we need because You love us. Help me teach them in a way they can understand that Your Word says to "seek first the kingdom of God and His righteousness, and all these things shall be added to you" (Matthew 6:33). And to "taste and *see that the LORD is good*; blessed is the man who trusts in Him!" (Psalm 34:8). Also that "*there is no want to those who fear Him*" (verse 9). And "*those who seek the LORD shall not lack any good thing*" (verse 10).

Help me to explain to them that You are always

close to them, and they are never alone. And You care so much about every detail of their lives that You want them to talk to You in prayer every day.

In Jesus' name I pray.

God's Word to Me

In this the love of God was manifested toward us,
that God has sent His only begotten Son into the world,
that we might live through Him.

1 John 4:9

I am persuaded that neither death nor life,
nor angels nor principalities nor powers,
nor things present nor things to come,
nor height nor depth, nor any other created thing,
shall be able to separate us from the love of God
which is in Christ Jesus our Lord.

Romans 8:38-39

There is no fear in love; but perfect love casts out fear,
because fear involves torment. But he who fears has not
been made perfect in love.

1 John 4:18

"Am I a God near at hand," says the Lord,
"and not a God afar off?"

Jeremiah 23:23

That Christ may dwell in your hearts through faith;
that you, being rooted and grounded in love,
may be able to comprehend…
the love of Christ which passes knowledge;
that you may be filled with all the fullness of God.

Ephesians 3:17-19

4

Lord, Instruct My Grandchildren to Honor Their Father and Mother

*T*he fifth of the Ten Commandments says, "Honor your father and your mother, *that your days may be long upon the land which the LORD your God is giving you*" (Exodus 20:12).

Paul said, "*Children, obey your parents in the Lord, for this is right.* 'Honor your father and mother,' *which is the first commandment with promise: 'that it may be well with you and you may live long on the earth'*" (Ephesians 6:1-3).

We all want our grandchildren to live well and long. That's why children must be taught to honor their parents.

It's the parents' responsibility to insist on respect from their children, but some parents don't do that. The children rule the house instead of the parents. This is why we must pray that the parents of our grandchildren will recognize any continued disobedience, rudeness, or unacceptable behavior in their child is a sign that they disrespect the parents' authority and should not be tolerated. The parents who allow this are doing a disservice to their children and setting them up for many problems in their future.

Pray that your grandchildren will be taught to be respectful and obedient to their parents and not allowed to talk or act disrespectfully toward them. The Bible says, "He who mistreats his father and chases away his mother is a son who causes shame and brings reproach" (Proverbs 19:26). Of course, parents must be loving, kind, fair, and trustworthy toward their children so they understand that just as God knows what is best for them, so do their parents.

If you have a grandchild who is already displaying a disrespectful attitude toward his or her parents, pray for God to intervene. Ask God for an opening to explain to the child that respect and obedience are requirements from God for *everyone* because He wants what is best for us. God says to *all* of us—even as adults—that if we want a long and good life, we must honor our parents.

If either of the parents of your grandchild have shown disrespect for *you*, pray for conviction to come into his or her heart about that—and even a confession before God. An apology to you wouldn't be a bad thing either, but don't push it. Dropping reminders is probably not a good idea. You can, instead, demonstrate your skill at forgiving and moving on and let God deal with the rest.

Do whatever you can to instill love and respect in your grandchildren for their mother and father.

Ask God to show you how to reinforce the rules the parents have laid down, even though you might be tempted not to do so. You may have to do battle in prayer first in order to resist any attitude in your grandchild that is not honoring to his or her parents. And you may have to resist any similar attitude in yourself as well if you don't agree with what the parents are requiring. Ask God to be in charge of that situation so that any thoughts of dishonor or disrespect will be eliminated.

Remember, the job of the mother and father is to be the parents and discipline and raise their children. It is our job is to be the grandparents and think that the grandchildren are perfect no matter what they do.

Even if a parent has done things that are not deserving of honor, God still requires that the children don't do anything to dishonor them. They don't have to be best friends with an abusive parent, but they can give honor from afar for at least giving them life. That is, unless the grandchildren have been handed to you to raise. If that happens, get kneepads and pray that those children will obey and honor you as they would any parent.

My Prayer to God

Lord, I lift up my grandchildren to You. (<u>Name each grandchild before God.</u>) I pray that You would teach them to honor their parents. Help their parents to understand why it is important to require that of their children and not allow them to rule the family. Expose the parents to all You say about this in Your Word. Give them understanding as to how important this is to their children's quality and length of life.

Give each of my grandchildren a humble heart that receives instruction and doesn't constantly push back against it. I know that every child will test the boundaries, so I pray that the parents will make the boundaries clear. Give each parent the ability to be consistent with his or her rules and requirements without being hardhearted and loveless. Give them love and the ability to care responsibly for their children so that their children don't become frustrated and angry.

Give each of my grandchildren the desire to live a long and good life that comes by honoring his or her father and mother, which also honors You. Help me to encourage them to do that, and show me ways I can reinforce that attitude of respect.

When my grandchildren stay with me, help me to honor their parents' instructions and requests so that I never encourage them to be disobedient in any way to their parents' rules and requirements. Give me words that build up who their parents are and how much they deserve respect. If any one of my grandchildren is grown up and forgiveness is needed between him and his parents, I pray You would open the door for that. Enable me to encourage this restoration to happen. If nothing like that has happened in my grandchild's family, I pray it never will.

In Jesus' name I pray.

God's Word to Me

Children, obey your parents in all things,
for this is well pleasing to the Lord.

COLOSSIANS 3:20

Whoever curses his father or his mother,
his lamp will be put out in deep darkness.

PROVERBS 20:20

The eye that mocks his father,
and scorns obedience to his mother,
the ravens of the valley will pick it out,
and the young eagles will eat it.

PROVERBS 30:17

Those who sat in darkness and in the shadow of death,
bound in affliction and irons—because
they rebelled against the words of God,
and despised the counsel of the Most High,
therefore He brought down their heart with labor;
they fell down, and there was none to help.

PSALM 107:10-12

Listen to your father who begot you,
and do not despise your mother when she is old.

PROVERBS 23:22

5

Lord, Give Each of My Grandchildren a Heart That Is Quick to Forgive

*O*ur grandchildren need to understand that *all* of God's commandments and rules are for our own good and given because He loves us. When we keep His rules, our lives work better. For example, God wants us to be forgiving because when we are not forgiving, we are the ones who are tortured by it.

When Peter asked Jesus how many times he needed to forgive someone, Jesus essentially said, "As many times as it takes." (See Matthew 18:21-22.) Then He gave an example of a king who forgave his servant a *huge* debt he owed, but that same servant went out and refused to forgive a fellow servant who owed him a *small* debt.

When the king found out what his servant did, he "was angry, and *delivered him to the torturers* until he should pay all that was due to him" (Matthew 18:34). Jesus said, "*So My heavenly Father also will do to you if each of you, from his heart, does not forgive his brother his trespasses*" (verse 35).

It doesn't get any clearer than that. God has forgiven us. We must forgive others.

When we don't forgive others the way our heavenly Father God forgives us, we become tortured in our soul. No one escapes it. And that torture will not stop until we forgive. Unforgiveness stops our life from flowing the way it should. It makes us miserable because it comes between God and us until we let the offense go.

Pray that your grandchildren will not only learn to be forgiving people, but that they will also be *quick* to forgive. The longer they take to forgive, the greater the toll on their body, mind, emotions, and life. Hanging on to unforgiveness means they won't be able to truly move on in their lives until they get rid of it. People who don't let go of offenses quickly are destined to not move beyond where they are. And not only that, they will suffer in some way physically, mentally, and spiritually.

There are too many broken families, and broken relationships in families, because people were not taught to forgive. Some people grow up and break all ties with their siblings, parents, or other family members because of a heart that refuses to forgive an offense. That kind of disobedience is not worth the torturous consequences for it. If you know of anything like that in your family, or the families of your grandchildren, your prayers can make a big difference.

Your prayers can help to soften people's hearts so they can better hear from God about the need for forgiveness.

Jesus said, "*Whatever you bind on earth will be bound in heaven,* and *whatever you loose on earth will be loosed in heaven*" (Matthew 18:18). I used to wonder about what it would be like to meet someone in heaven who had done something bad to you or your family, but who later repented, received Jesus, and entered heaven when he died. If you had not forgiven him on earth, could it be that this would be a problem for you and not for him when you get to heaven? Whatever the answer is to that question, it's better to take care of unforgiveness as soon as possible.

Jesus said, "Whenever you stand praying, *if you have anything against anyone, forgive him, that your Father in heaven may also forgive you your trespasses*" (Mark 11:25). That means before we even pray we should forgive anyone we have not yet fully forgiven. For some of us who have repeat offenders in our lives, we may have to forgive the same person many times. As Jesus implied—as long as it takes.

Jesus also said that if we don't forgive others, God won't forgive us. That is a very serious problem. It means there are crucial things that will not flow into our lives if we do not forgive other people.

Determine to be a godly example of a forgiving person to your grandchildren. Ask God to show you if you need to forgive anyone for something that happened in the past, even as recently as yesterday. We don't want our children and grandchildren to inherit a spirit of bitterness flowing out from us. Unforgiveness can be a family trait. We've all seen families where *not* forgiving others is perpetuated. Be determined that it *won't* be perpetuated in *you* or *your* family. Become a prayer warrior who prays against any lack of forgiveness in your children and grandchildren so they can move into everything God has for them.

Forgiveness is an act of love that we give—whether the other person deserves it or not—because God out of His love has forgiven us.

Children can learn to forgive as soon as they are able to understand what that means. It helps if they see forgiveness modeled in their parents. But if not, it can still be modeled for them in you. Because we leave a spiritual inheritance for our children and grandchildren (see chapter 8), it behooves us to forgive anyone and everyone we need to so that unforgiveness doesn't become a habit we can't break.

One of the greatest benefits of knowing God is that He forgives all of our sins and releases us from the consequences of them. He asks us to forgive others. That frees us from the torturous consequences of *not* forgiving.

It's the least we can do for all God has done for us.

My Prayer to God

Lord, I lift up my grandchildren to You. (<u>Name each grandchild before God.</u>) I pray that each of them will have a heart that is quick to forgive. Let no root of bitterness creep into the heart of any grandchild because he or she refused to let an offense go. Help my grandchildren to understand how far-reaching Your love, mercy, and forgiveness are, and how much You want them to be loving, merciful, and forgiving to others.

Reveal any place in my heart and mind where I have not forgiven someone or have placed blame for something bad that happened and not let go of it. I don't want to carry excess baggage around with me that will keep my prayers from being answered and hinder my receiving all the blessings You have for me. And I don't want my grandchildren to inherit any kind of negative family trait that will keep them from moving into all You have for *them*.

Help their parents to be forgiving people as well. Where there is any lack of forgiveness in their hearts—especially toward each other—I pray You would bring that stronghold of torture down to nothing. Cause them to refuse to perpetuate it any longer. Open their hearts to recognize the damage unforgiveness causes and help them to determine not to live that way any longer.

Make me to be a good and godly influence on my grandchildren. Show me how to guide them in the way of love, mercy, and forgiveness. Teach them to learn to forgive *quickly* and *completely* so they are never tortured by unforgiveness—and Your plan for their lives is never hindered.

In Jesus' name I pray.

God's Word to Me

If you do not forgive men their trespasses,
neither will your Father forgive your trespasses.

MATTHEW 6:15

I say to you, love your enemies,
bless those who curse you,
do good to those who hate you,
and pray for those who spitefully use you
and persecute you,
that you may be sons of your Father in heaven.

MATTHEW 5:44-45

Forgive us our debts,
as we forgive our debtors.

MATTHEW 6:12

Bless the LORD, O my soul,
and forget not all His benefits:
who forgives all your iniquities,
who heals all your diseases.

PSALM 103:2-3

Be kind to one another, tenderhearted,
forgiving one another,
just as God in Christ forgave you.

EPHESIANS 4:32

6

Lord, Teach My Grandchildren Ways to Show Their Love for You

We have all known people—both adults and children—who are complainers. They find little for which they are grateful. They complain every day about something instead of seeing what is good in their lives. They are unhappy and miserable. Their glass is always half empty instead of half full. We don't want that for our grandchildren. Never being thankful for what they have leads to a miserable life that will keep them from moving into all God has for them.

Having a grateful heart will serve a child well for his or her entire life.

Pray for your grandchildren to know God, understand His love for them, and trust Him to take care of them. Being dependent upon God for everything and grateful for all He does for them every day creates a heart of thanksgiving. Pray also that they will learn how to express their love for Him with thanks and praise, so they can see how that attitude opens up their life to all the wonderful blessings He has for them.

All this, of course, is learned more and more in each stage and development of a child's life. A three-year-old can thank God for his food and family and pets, for example. A nine-year-old can choose to praise God and thank Him for her parents, friends, teachers, and home. A thirteen-year-old can choose to praise God as the Giver of all that is good in life—such as love, guidance, protection, friends, and health. The Bible says to "give thanks to the Lord, for He is good!" and because "His mercy endures forever" (Psalm 136:1). God's goodness and mercy alone are all the reasons we need to worship Him.

A heart of thankfulness and praise, instead of a spirit of complaint and entitlement, opens the channels through which God's blessings flow into our lives.

The first step toward being a grateful person is knowing that God is good—*all the time*. Being able to reinforce that truth to your grandchildren is vitally important for them. Teaching them to recognize all that is good in their lives every day and saying, "Thank You, God, for all that" is a powerful thing. And teaching them that even when something bad happens, God is still good, gives them countless reasons for which to thank Him.

I taught my daughter and son to look at a situation they were concerned about and say, "What is good about this situation?" Finding the good and thanking God for it leads to a praise-filled heart. And that is a heart God wants to fill with more of His love, peace, joy, beauty, and power. In other words, more of Himself.

Who doesn't need that?

This is such an important issue for our grandchildren. Being grateful to God anchors their heart closer to Him. And when they are plugged into Him so *His* life is in *them*, they are dwelling in *His* kingdom.

Pray especially that your grandchildren will grow up appreciating who God made them to be. Always comparing themselves to someone else and feeling as if they fall short is a setup for disaster—especially among siblings. Each child is unique and has special talents and abilities, and they need to be assured of that. Often parents are too busy to do this alone, so you can be the one to reinforce that each grandchild is unique and God has great plans and purposes for that child. (More about that in chapters 24 and 25.)

Your constant and consistent reinforcement of each grandchild's personhood and value will encourage that child to be thankful for who they are. Directing them to express their thanks to God for everything can create in them a heart of praise and worship—and help them grow into people who are habitually thankful every day.

Your prayers for your grandchildren about this will affect their lives forever. It can take the burden of feeling inadequate off them—or never allow it to come near them in the first place—and help them appreciate who God made them to be. A heart of worship is a heart that welcomes everything God wants to pour into his or her life.

The Bible says, "Although they knew God, they did not glorify Him as God, *nor were thankful, but became futile in their thoughts, and their foolish hearts were darkened*" (Romans 1:21). We don't want our grandchildren thinking futile and foolish thoughts because they were not taught to be thankful to God.

The Bible also says, "*Let us continually offer the sacrifice of praise to God*, that is, the fruit of our lips, giving thanks to His name" (Hebrews 13:15).

So let's do this. Starting with *us*. Let's thank and praise God so frequently that it penetrates the hearts of those around us—especially our grandchildren.

My Prayer to God

Lord, I lift up my grandchildren to You. (Name each grandchild before God.) Help them to understand how good You are—all the time. Help them to learn how You forgive us, heal us, save us from destruction, show us kindness, and are always loving and merciful toward us. (See Psalm 103.) Help each grandchild to understand who You really are so that they will learn to love You above all else. I pray that the clear knowledge of who You are will cause them to never allow anyone or anything to come between them and their love for You. Help them to think of You as their greatest treasure so that they will make room in their heart for You, and in their life for all You have for them.

Your Word says, "One generation shall praise Your works to another, and shall declare Your mighty acts" (Psalm 145:4). I pray that You will help me speak of my gratefulness for You to my grandchildren for all You have done for *me*—as well as for *them*. Help me to express to them my praise to You for all that You are and all You do so they will learn to imitate that attitude. I pray that if any one of my grandchildren has a tendency to complain or not be grateful, change that child's heart to one of thanksgiving. Show me how I can encourage him or her to do that.

Teach my grandchildren to make room in their heart for Your love by daily expressing *their* love for You. Thank You that as they praise You, it opens up their heart for You to pour more of Your love, joy, and peace into them.

Your Word says, "Where your treasure is, there your heart will be also" (Matthew 6:21). Help my grandchildren to make You their greatest treasure. Enable me to teach them that we love You because You "first loved us," and loving You is the first and most important thing we do in our lives (1 John 4:19).

In Jesus' name I pray.

God's Word to Me

You shall love the LORD your God with all your heart,
with all your soul, with all your mind,
and with all your strength.
This is the first commandment.

MARK 12:30

Because Your lovingkindness is better than life,
my lips shall praise You.
Thus I will bless You while I live;
I will lift up my hands in Your name.

PSALM 63:3-4

It is good to give thanks to the LORD,
and to sing praises to Your name, O Most High;
to declare Your lovingkindness in the morning,
and Your faithfulness every night.

PSALM 92:1-2

Offer to God thanksgiving,
and pay your vows to the Most High.
Call upon Me in the day of trouble;
I will deliver you, and you shall glorify Me.

PSALM 50:14-15

I will praise You with my whole heart...
for Your lovingkindness and Your truth.

PSALM 138:1-2

7

Lord, Reveal to My Grandchildren How to Love Others the Way You Do

God wants us to love others the same way He loves us—unconditionally, unfailingly, and perfectly. But this is not possible on our own. Human love is imperfect, fickle, and it fails.

But God's love is perfect. It never fails. That's why we need the love of God in us in order to love others. Jesus said, "This is My commandment, that *you love one another as I have loved you*" (John 15:12). He also said that loving Him and loving others were the two greatest commandments.

Jesus said, "*If you keep My commandments, you will abide in My love,* just as I have kept My Father's commandments and abide in His love. These things I have spoken to you, that My joy may remain in you, and *that your joy may be full*" (John 15:10-11). In other words, when we live God's way, we live in His love, and that gives us joy and fulfillment.

God says our love for others is the sign that we know Him. It's one of the fruit of His Spirit living in us. The more time we spend with God in His Word, in prayer, and in praise and worship, the more of His love can be found in our heart. That means we have more love to extend to others.

The Bible says, "No one has seen God at any time. If we love one another, God abides in us, and His love has been perfected in us" (1 John 4:12). This means that although no one has actually seen God, people can see Him in *us* whenever we extend love to *them*. Loving others pleases God and gives meaning to our lives. But we cannot truly love others until we first love God and receive His love for us. Jesus gave us a way to love others by His Spirit of love living in us, and then as we express our love to Him, His love grows in us and overflows to other people.

One of the ways we show our love for God is by loving other people with the love He puts in our hearts.

When Jesus talked about being perfect the way our "Father in heaven is perfect," He was talking about *loving others the way God does* (Matthew 5:48). That means fully, unconditionally, mercifully, without criticism, and with no judgment. We can only love others that way because of His perfect love in our hearts produced by the Holy Spirit of love in us.

Loving others doesn't mean loving God's enemy, but we can still have love for someone who is *influenced* by God's enemy. And we can show that love by praying that their heart will be broken by God and opened to the truth of who He is.

Because of the love of God in us, enabling our prayers, we can develop a love for people we never thought we could.

God wants us to "put on love, which is the bond of perfection" (Colossians 3:14). This is something we decide to do and deliberately do it.

We can pray that each one of our grandchildren will have a heart of love for their family members, friends, and others. We can help them see that they have a choice to make with regard to loving others. They can deliberately choose to obey God and love others. And they can ask God to help them do that.

Teach your grandchildren that love is *patient* and *kind*. It is not envious. It doesn't show off, and it isn't prideful, rude, selfish, easily annoyed, or annoying. Love doesn't think bad thoughts or celebrate someone's suffering. Love seeks the well-being of others. (See 1 Corinthians 13:4-8 and 1 Corinthians 10:23-24.) If we see our children, grandchildren, or even ourselves acting or thinking in any of those negative ways, that means we have not chosen to love others with the love God has given us.

A child who has God's love in their heart for others will prosper.

We want our grandchildren to succeed in life, so we must pray that they learn to love others the way He does.

My Prayer to God

Lord, I lift up my grandchildren to You. (<u>Name each grandchild before God.</u>) I ask that You would put love in each child's heart for other people, especially for his or her family members and friends, but also for people who are not easy to love. Help my grandchildren to learn to love others the way You do. Help us all as a family to forsake envy, pride, rudeness, selfishness, and criticism —which reveal a lack of love for others—so we can learn to "walk in love, as Christ also has loved us" (Ephesians 5:2).

Teach my grandchildren to understand Your commandment to love others. Let their love for others be the most important sign that they know You, love You, and serve You. Show them if there is any way they show a lack of love to others. Help them see that the things they do without love will not be blessed by You, but the things they do that are born out of love will last forever.

Enable my grandchildren to understand that love is what gives meaning to everything they do. Help them know that one of the greatest gifts of love they can give anyone is to pray for them. If there is ever a friend, family member, acquaintance, or neighbor who is troubling or hateful to them, teach them to pray for that person and release them into Your hands. Instead of thinking of retribution, show them that praying for those difficult people to have a life-changing encounter with You is actually the best revenge. Grow each of my grandchildren to be a person whose heart is filled to overflowing with Your love for other people. Help me to always model that as well.

In Jesus' name I pray.

God's Word to Me

Above all things have fervent love for one another,
for "love will cover a multitude of sins."

1 PETER 4:8

Let no one seek his own,
but each one the other's well-being.

1 CORINTHIANS 10:24

This commandment we have from Him:
that he who loves God must love his brother also.

1 JOHN 4:21

He who hates his brother is in darkness
and walks in darkness,
and does not know where he is going,
because the darkness has blinded his eyes.

1 JOHN 2:11

Just as you want men to do to you,
you also do to them likewise.

LUKE 6:31

Praying for Your Grandchildren's Safety and Protection

8

Lord, Teach Me to See the Inheritance I Leave as a Praying Grandparent

From the moment you hear you are going to be a grandparent, you have great joy. Someone new to love will enter your life and forever impact it. You may have been doing important things before, but now they will all take a backseat to this great addition. You are thrilled and happy as you go to bed that night, but in the morning you may wake up with what-if thoughts.

What if the baby's mother is unable to carry the baby? What if she gets sick? What if she has an accident? What if there is something wrong in the baby's development? What if my grandchild is molested or hurt by some evil person? What if the child cannot attend a good school in a safe area?

These kinds of thoughts are endless, and they quickly convince you that you have no control over any of that. You have to exert the influence God gives you in prayer and pray for protection.

But where do you start when there is so much to pray about?

Start in God's Word. It is encouraging, life giving, and faith building.

The opening verses just before the beginning of this book say that the benefits of the Lord's righteousness in those of us who love and serve Him are extended to our "children's children"—our grandchildren—as well (Psalm 103:17). The Bible tells us that the way we live affects not only *our* happiness and well-being, but also that of our children and grandchildren. The Bible says, "*He has blessed your children* within you" (Psalm 147:13). And "*their descendants will be established before You*" (Psalm 102:28). It says, "In the fear of the LORD there is strong confidence, and *His children will have a place of refuge*" (Proverbs 14:26). That means because we have the fear of the Lord in us, we have a place of protection and hope in Him that can also be extended to our children and grandchildren.

The opposite is promised to those who do *not* love God and live His way. This is the way God describes Himself: "The LORD God, merciful and gracious, longsuffering, and abounding in goodness and truth…forgiving iniquity and transgression and sin, by no means clearing the guilty, *visiting the iniquity of the fathers upon the children and the children's children* to the third and the fourth generation" (Exodus 34:6-7).

This is a frightening warning to those who choose to live without God. This doesn't mean that every time we do something wrong our children will suffer. Our repentance and refusal to *keep doing it* spares them. When we live with reverence and love for God and His ways, we leave a spiritual inheritance to our grandchildren. "*A good man leaves an inheritance to his children's children*" (Proverbs 13:22).

The Bible says that we who have received God are His

children. "The Spirit Himself bears witness with our spirit that *we are children of God, and if children, then heirs—heirs of God and joint heirs with Christ* " (Romans 8:16-17). That is a rich inheritance for us, and one that affects the lives of our children and grandchildren as well.

Don't be put off by the word "man" in Proverbs 13:22. That doesn't mean a *grandmother's* prayers don't count. Insert the word "person" in there. Or think of the word "mankind," which is what we say to represent all men and women. The point is, our relationship with God affects our children and grandchildren. It doesn't take the place of their own personal relationship with God. They are still accountable for that. And it doesn't mean if something bad happens to one of our grand-children, it's our fault. It means that our own obedience to God has blessings for our descendants connected to it.

God's Presence, Grandchildren, and Other Addictions

You may be thinking, *I have not always lived God's way.* Or, *I have only recently come to know the Lord.* Or, *I have never really received Jesus into my heart. Do these promises still apply to me?* Yes, they do. That's because it is never too late to begin a relationship with the Lord. Simply pray, "Dear Jesus, I believe You are the Son of God, who died in my place to pay the price for my sins. And You rose again from the dead to guarantee that I can have life with You forever in eternity and a better life here on earth. Forgive me of all my sins and help me to live Your way now."

Once you have prayed that prayer and received Jesus, His Spirit lives in your heart. You now have access to His presence every time you pray or worship Him. His presence will bring about a wonderful fulfillment of who you were made to be.

You will become so addicted to His wonderful, healing, and comforting presence that you won't ever want to live without it.

Receiving Jesus also means that from now on you can be free from bad addictions to wrong behavior. As long as you live His way and depend totally on Him, He will enable you to rise above the things in your life that are not His will for you. He will help you to live the life He died for you to have—a life of blessing, hope, and purpose.

Grandchildren are some of God's greatest blessings, and it's very easy to become addicted to them. Always thinking about them and wanting to be with them is a *good* addiction. God's presence and grandchildren are two addictions that will forever bring you joy.

If you have inherited grandchildren through marriage—either you married someone who already had children and grandchildren, or your child married someone who already had children, the situation can be delicate. I want you to know that your prayers can still positively affect the lives of those involved. You can pray the same prayers in this book for them, but ask the Holy Spirit for guidance about how to pray specifically for these fragile family relationships. Ask Him to show you ways you can be a blessing. And don't entertain the expectations that these people will always act the way you want them to. That is a setup for hurt feelings. Ask God to open their hearts to you if they seem closed. Only He can do that. Just keep praying these prayers and asking God to mend all relationships where they are broken.

Keep in mind that being a praying grandparent is not just a good thing to do, it is a calling, a privilege, and a commitment. Whether your connection to your grandchildren is biological, or if they have come by adoption, or you inherited them through a marriage—whether you see them often or not at all—they will always need your prayers. If it ever seems as if they do not deserve your prayers, then pray anyway, simply because it is God's will and it pleases Him.

Praying for your grandchildren is a lifelong ministry for you. You have no idea how far-reaching, powerful, and effective your prayers are. God not only hears your prayers and will answer them, but He will *continue answering* them long after you have gone to be with Him. They can affect generations after you for His glory.

Start by praying that every generation—from your children and grandchildren on—will know Jesus as their Lord and Savior and live for Him.

We don't know when the Lord will return, so don't stop praying until you see Him. Your prayers for your grandchildren will be an important aspect of your grandchildren's safety and protection. They will be the best inheritance you can leave them because they will last a lifetime—yours and theirs.

Because you have lived longer and can see the bigger picture—while parents are focused on the daily details of life, which they must be—you can see life from a broader perspective. *God's* perspective.

And *God's* perspective will always guide your prayers.

My Prayer to God

Lord, I lift up my grandchildren to You. (Name each grandchild before God.) Help me to clearly see the spiritual inheritance I leave each one when I pray for them. Thank You for all of the wonderful promises in Your Word that declare You will bless my children and grandchildren when I live Your way. I know that children are a gift from You and grandchildren are a crown of glory upon my life (Proverbs 17:6). I know that whether I can see my grandchildren often or not, I can still be close to them every time I pray for them.

Thank You that You hear "the prayer of the righteous" (Proverbs 15:29). I am righteous because I have received You, Jesus, and I love and serve You. Thank You that my prayers for my grandchildren are lasting, so that when I have left this earth to be with You, the effects of my prayers will still be felt.

Your Word says my children and *their* children "will be established before You" (Psalm 102:28). I know that "a good man leaves an inheritance to his children's children" (Proverbs 13:22). Thank You that there is an inheritance I can leave my children and grandchildren that is even more valuable than possessions, and that precious gift is a spiritual inheritance that will help them to be established on a good foundation.

Help me to live Your way, confessing it to You when I haven't, so that I am clean before You. Enable me to fulfill my calling to pray—especially for my children and grandchildren. Thank You that I am called "to an inheritance incorruptible and undefiled and that does not fade away, reserved in heaven" (1 Peter 1:4). Help me to live in obedience to Your commandments so that I can leave a great spiritual inheritance to my children and grandchildren.

In Jesus' name I pray.

God's Word to Me

You are no longer a slave but a son, and if a son,
then an heir of God through Christ.

GALATIANS 4:7

In Him also we have obtained an inheritance,
being predestined according to the purpose of
Him who works all things
according to the counsel of His will.

EPHESIANS 1:11

The silver-haired head is a crown of glory,
if it is found in the way of righteousness.

PROVERBS 16:31

Giving thanks to the Father who has qualified us to be
partakers of the inheritance of the saints in the light.

COLOSSIANS 1:12

Not returning evil for evil or reviling for reviling,
but on the contrary blessing,
knowing that you were called to this,
that you may inherit a blessing.

1 PETER 3:9

9

Lord, Help My Grandchildren's Parents to Raise Them Your Way

very parent needs prayer. They always have. But today there are so many unthinkably frightening challenges in the world that raising and preparing children to meet these challenges becomes a daunting task. No matter how difficult our lives may have been when we raised *our* children, the dangers are far worse in their generation than they ever were in ours. Raising their own children safely can seem overwhelming to them. The parents of your grandchildren need your prayer support. That's why you may at times find yourself praying almost as much for the *parents* as you are for your grandchildren.

It may be that one of the best gifts you give your grandchildren is to pray for their parents.

First of all, pray that the peace of God will rule their home and that the parents will be in unity about raising their children. This is especially important if the parents are divorced, which is always a touchy situation—and even more so if one parent wants to be his or her child's favorite no matter how he or she achieves that.

The Bible says to bring up a child God's way because then the child will end up living according to God's laws (Proverbs 22:6). But too often children are not brought up according to God's way. So pray first of all that your son, son-in-law, daughter, or daughter-in-law—as well as your grandchildren's stepparents, if any—know the Lord. If they do not know Jesus, pray they will open their heart to receive Him. Do not stop praying about that. If they already know the Lord, pray that they will grow stronger in their relationship with Him, and that their faith will be solid and ever-increasing. The spiritual life and nature of the parents will in countless ways determine whether their children end up on the right path or not.

Pray that the parents will teach their children well about God and His ways, and that they will be able to set a good example in that regard. God said of His commandments, "These words which I command you today shall be in your heart. *You shall teach them diligently to your children, and shall talk of them when you sit in your house*, when you walk by the way, when you lie down, and when you rise up" (Deuteronomy 6:6-7). In other words, morning, noon, and night. Constantly. Ongoingly. (More about that in chapter 16.)

If you did not raise your children God's way, and you feel that you made mistakes and can now see the consequence of them in your children, know that God is a Redeemer. He redeems all things. Don't forever beat yourself up over this. God's mercies are new every morning, so start fresh today and bring all of that before the Lord, asking Him to forgive you where forgiveness is needed. Ask Him to redeem all that has been lost. Commit yourself to pray for your children to open their lives to the Lord and live God's way now. Your prayers can reverse the way things are headed.

Be patient and keep praying. Turning a big ship around takes time.

Wisdom in Discipline

A big part of praying that the parents of your grandchildren will be able to care for and raise their children properly is to pray that they have wisdom in disciplining them. Too much or too little discipline can set up a child for problems.

God holds parents responsible to raise their children with love, guidance, and godly discipline. They must see to it that the children will have a right attitude that is built on a solid foundation of love and instruction. That means they should not try to "teach" by being critical of their children or making their children feel that they never live up to high expectations. Parents should not cause their children to feel abandoned, afraid, or hopeless in any way. When children grow up with those kinds of negative emotions, they have a hard time learning what they need to learn. That's because they must first learn how to survive. So pray that the parents will train their children to be obedient, and that they will know how to discipline their children with love when they are not.

Just as parents cannot be too harsh and merciless with their children, they can't be too lenient and careless. Either extreme produces a bad result. If too harsh, the children can be damaged in their spirit and will rebel against that at some point. If too lenient, they are left to do whatever they want, seemingly without consequences, and that deception can lead them to ruin. The Bible says, "Children, obey your parents in the Lord, for this is right" (Ephesians 6:1). It also says that children are to be *lovingly trained* and not provoked to frustration and anger. (See Ephesians 6:4.)

Proper discipline balanced with love is one of the greatest paths to safety for your grandchildren, because if they are disobedient to their parents, life will not go well for them. The Bible says, "Correct your son, and he will give you rest; yes, he will give delight to your soul" (Proverbs 29:17). You and their parents can only have peace about your grandchildren if they are properly corrected in love.

The Bible also says that parents who truly love their children will discipline them "promptly" (Proverbs 13:24). Learning that there are immediate consequences for disobedience can save a child's life.

Pray that your grandchildren are also taught to follow the instructions of others whom God puts in authority in their lives—such as teachers and law enforcement officers.

God promised David, "*If your sons will keep My covenant and My testimony which I shall teach them*, their sons also shall sit upon your throne forevermore" (Psalm 132:12). God promised David that his children would be blessed, and their children as well, if they lived God's way. Unfortunately, David did not diligently teach his children to follow after the Lord. Nor did he discipline them properly. He was too lenient, and they paid a severe and ultimate price for their ungodly actions.

Pray that your grandchildren's parents are encouraging, caring, patient, and lovingly affectionate to their children.

Pray also that your grandchildren's parents do what they need to do to keep their children out of bad schools and away from bad people and influences. A bad school, and a bad area in which to live, can mean the difference between life and death, success and failure, for a child.

Children are a gift from God, but not everyone sees them that way. "Behold, *children are a heritage from the* LORD, *the fruit of the womb is a reward.* Like arrows in the hand of a warrior, so are the children of one's youth. Happy is the man who has his quiver full of them" (Psalm 127:3-5). Pray that your grandchildren's parents will see their children as gifts from God.

Children belong to God, and He gives them to us to be entrusted to our care. They are important to Him, and He looks down on anyone who mistreats them. Pray that your grandchildren's parents will be instilled with the fear of God because "the fear of the LORD is a fountain of life, to turn one away from the snares of death" (Proverbs 14:27).

Loving and caring for children is one of the ways we honor God and build His kingdom. Pray that your grandchildren's parents will not be too busy to raise their children God's way. Pray they will see that raising their children God's way will not only honor Him, but it will also help to build His kingdom on earth.

My Prayer to God

Lord, I lift my grandchildren's parents, stepparents, or guardians up to You. (<u>Name each one before God.</u>) I pray that they will know how to teach each child to obey not only them, but also all who are in authority in their lives, such as teachers and law enforcement people. Instruct the parents to live Your way so that they can teach their children to live Your way as well. I pray that if a parent does not know You, You will open his or her mind to see Your truth and open his or her heart to receive Your life. Teach my grandchildren's parents Your laws and enable them to teach Your ways to their children as well.

Where I have failed in any way to raise my own children according to Your laws, forgive me for that. It was never my intention. Show me any wrong attitude I have had or actions I have committed so I can confess it all as sin before You. Whatever errors I have made in raising my children, help me to see them clearly. I pray You would keep any failure on my part from affecting my children or grandchildren now.

If my son or daughter, son-in-law or daughter-in-law, is not living Your way, I pray You would strike that parent's conscience and bring him or her to repentance before You so that the air can be cleared. Lift all blinders from his or her eyes so everything You have done can be clearly seen.

Send believers into each parent's life to influence

them for Your glory. Take away any bad influences so that they are not led away from Your kingdom. Free them from any addictions, bad habits, or ungodly behavior so that they will be good role models for their children.

Enable my grandchildren's parents to realize that they cannot raise their children well without You. Enable them to know how to discipline their children promptly in love and in proper ways. Help them not to be too lenient so that their children become spoiled and unruly. And keep them from being too strict so that their children's hearts and spirits are not broken.

Give the parents godly wisdom so they can make good decisions regarding each child. I pray they will invite You to be in charge of their children and seek Your help to bring them up in Your ways. Instruct them to teach their children Your Word so that they will live a long and good life. (See Deuteronomy 11:18-21.)

Cause the parents of my grandchildren to communicate well with one another so that they are in unity regarding the raising of their children. I pray they will each have the best interest of the children in their heart and mind and not try to undermine proper instruction by doing or allowing things to gain the children's affection away from the other parent. Give each parent a heart to serve You above all else.

In Jesus' name I pray.

God's Word to Me

Train up a child in the way he should go,
and when he is old he will not depart from it.

PROVERBS 22:6

You shall lay up these words of mine in
your heart and in your soul…
You shall teach them to your children,
speaking of them when you sit in your house,
when you walk by the way, when you lie down,
and when you rise up.
And you shall write them on the doorposts of
your house and on your gates,
that your days and the days of
your children may be multiplied.

DEUTERONOMY 11:18-21

Fathers, do not provoke your children to wrath,
but bring them up in the training and
admonition of the Lord.

EPHESIANS 6:4

No good thing will He withhold
from those who walk uprightly.

PSALM 84:11

10

Lord, Protect My Grandchildren from Any Danger or Threat

We are all well aware of the many dangers in the world today. They are worse than we ever imagined they could be and found in places we never thought to be unsafe before—such as schools, movie theaters, restaurants, and malls. They are sometimes perpetrated by people we might never have thought to be so dangerously abnormal.

How do we begin to protect our children and grandchildren wherever they are? We can homeschool them and keep them out of theaters and malls, but even then there are still no guarantees. One day they have to go out in the world, and, as we have seen, disaster can happen anywhere.

Neither we nor their parents can protect our grandchildren from everything. Only God can do that.

We must pray daily for God's hand of protection to cover our grandchildren. Even when I take care of my grandchildren in my own home, I pray constantly that God will protect them and help me to recognize all possible dangers. I have two little ones under the age of two right now, and I can't take my eyes off them for even a second. The thought of something happening to one of them at any time is horrifying, but it would be unthinkable if it occurred on my watch. I'm always praying fervently about this. As we well know, accidents happen quickly and suddenly. So we must be praying ongoingly for God's protection on our grandchildren, as well as their parents, caretakers, other grandparents, or family members who help care for them.

Pray that your grandchildren will be safe in their own home. Freak accidents happen at home when least expected. That's because home is where we let down our guard and don't always see possible dangers ahead.

Pray that your grandchildren will be safe wherever they travel. Pray they will be safe in every car, plane, bus, or train they are traveling in. Pray for their safety wherever they ride a bicycle or walk—on every street and in every building they enter.

Pray for good and safe neighborhoods for your grandchildren to live in. Pray for godly neighbors. The Bible says, "Do not devise evil against your neighbor, *for he dwells by you for safety's sake*" (Proverbs 3:29). Good neighbors are a big part of your grandchildren's safety. If they are not in a safe neighborhood now, pray that they and their family will be able to move to one that is. Pray that any unseen dangers, wherever they are, will be exposed and not able to threaten your grandchildren at any time.

Pray there will be no sudden accidents. Each of my children had to be rushed to the emergency room for stitches in their forehead when they were about two years old, and each accident occurred right in front of me. I was no more than two feet away from them, and the situation happened so fast I could do nothing to stop it. Both of them made a sudden move I wasn't expecting. My son suddenly leaped on my bed and hit the headboard. My daughter started to run in a hotel room, and before I could even get the words "Don't run!" out of my mouth, she tripped and fell into the corner of a wall. I learned to always pray about sudden accidents after that.

Pray for your grandchildren to grow up with a great ability to sense danger. Ask God to enable them to know when something they are doing could be a danger to themselves or others. Having a sense of danger has spared my life countless times and the lives of my children as well. God gives us wisdom, insight, revelation, understanding, and common sense when we ask for that. And His Spirit speaks to us about what to do or not do.

God says when you turn to Him, "Your ears shall hear a word behind you, saying, 'This is the way, walk in it,' whenever you turn to the right hand or whenever you turn to the left" (Isaiah 30:21). Pray that your grandchildren are able to hear these words from God to their heart at an early age.

Still, as much as we pray and as hard as we try, accidents can happen. When they do, pray there will be no permanent damage and everyone will learn to be more cautious because of it. The truth is, only God can keep us and our children and grandchildren in the safety for which we long every day. Only God can protect us, and those for whom we pray, from unseen dangers lurking about. We must never stop praying about that.

All that being said, children can still become ill or injured, and some may die. It's one of life's heartbreaking and unthinkable realities. And there are many reasons that can happen, which are too extensive to go into now. But if it does happen, may we have the comfort of knowing that it was not because we didn't pray. And though our hearts are broken and the loss will be felt for a lifetime, we have the assurance that this precious child is with Jesus and we will see him or her again.

My Prayer to God

Lord, I pray for my grandchildren. (Name each grandchild before God.) I ask that You would put Your hand of protection upon them. Keep them safe from accidents or dangers of any kind. Surround them with Your angels. I know that "You alone" can make them to "dwell in safety" (Psalm 4:8). Help them to understand that You are their protector, and You can keep them safe when they live Your way and seek Your hand of protection. Enable them to see that when they go their own way, without regard for Your way, they walk out from under Your umbrella of protection.

Give my grandchildren the ability to sense danger—either to themselves or to others. Help them to hear Your voice speaking to their heart saying, "Walk *this* way, not *that* way." (See Isaiah 30:21.) Give them no peace about going anyplace, or doing anything, that will expose them or others to danger.

I pray that my grandchildren will always live in safe neighborhoods with godly neighbors. Teach them to be a blessing to their neighbors and to people in their school, workplace, and wherever they go. Where there are dangerous people around, I pray that none will come near to threaten them in any way. Expose the threats that bullies and bad people can impose on them, and remove these people from their surroundings. If necessary, I pray that my grandchildren and their family will be able to move to a safer neighborhood.

Keep all my grandchildren's parents, stepparents, caretakers, and everyone around them alert to possible dangers at all times. Give all who care for them the ability to see ahead what the dangers are. Whenever I'm around them, make me aware of all possible dangers as well. Show me anything I need to see. Keep my grandchildren safe in cars, planes, trains, buses, on bicycles, and in any other form of transportation. Keep them safe wherever they walk and in whatever activity they are involved in. Thank You, Lord, that I can have peace because I know that You protect us and help us to live safely when we pray and live Your way.

In Jesus' name I pray.

God's Word to Me

He shall give His angels charge over you,
to keep you in all your ways.

PSALM 91:11

You shall not be afraid of the terror by night,
nor of the arrow that flies by day,
nor of the pestilence that walks in darkness,
nor of the destruction that lays waste at noonday.
A thousand may fall at your side,
and ten thousand at your right hand;
but it shall not come near you.

PSALM 91:5-7

"For the oppression of the poor,
for the sighing of the needy,
now I will arise," says the LORD;
"I will set him in the safety for which he yearns."

PSALM 12:5

Because you have made the LORD,
who is my refuge,
even the Most High, your dwelling place,
no evil shall befall you,
nor shall any plague come near your dwelling.

PSALM 91:9-10

11

Lord, Heal My
Grandchildren from Every
Disease and Infirmity

*S*ickness can be the consequence of abusing our body and not taking care of ourself. When that is the case with our grandchildren, we can pray that they will be attracted to life-giving, health-sustaining food and have the knowledge and strength to resist whatever will harm them. This is an important prayer for them. With so many options and confusing information coming at them, pray they will always have access to the food they need to sustain good health and long life, and that they learn to make good choices. No matter what age they are, pray for your grandchildren to be led by God's Spirit with the care of their bodies.

Don't you wish someone had been praying for you about always making the best food choices? I know I do.

Pray that your grandchildren will always be able to resist poor eating habits—especially any kind of eating disorder. The daughter of one of my friends developed an eating disorder when she was about 14 years old. She was very attractive and talented, and she was appearing on television and in commercials in Hollywood. That meant she was often around situations where there was constant judgment on her appearance. I had known this girl since she was about eight, and she was a totally normal, sweet, and godly child. However, when she developed an eating disorder, her personality completely changed.

It was as if a bad spirit had taken over her mind. Whenever she was around food, or it was mealtime, she would repeat over and over, "I'm not hungry. I'm not hungry. I'm not hungry." And she wouldn't eat. Her parents were deeply concerned, especially because she was losing weight and got down to a dangerously low level. Her parents sought professional help. We often gathered with them and other strong believing parents to pray for their daughter until this was finally broken.

I suggested to the parents to get her out of the entertainment industry because constant comparison with others in that body image-obsessed culture was destroying her. They did just that because they knew they were fighting for her life.

They had wisdom and direction from God to take her on a couple of missions trips with their church. When she saw the extreme poverty and great physical and spiritual need of the people in the countries she visited, she began to change. Her compassionate heart kept her focus on helping people and serving God. She soon saw the deception she had fallen under by being so focused on herself. She eventually became totally free of the eating disorder and married a wonderful young man with the same heart to help others. They now work together as missionaries and love what they do.

Pray that your grandchildren are never attracted to any kind of eating disorder. This is as much a spiritual battle as it is a mental, emotional, and physical one. Body image obsession is a deadly idol the enemy uses to destroy our children. Stand strong against this evil deception that can weave its way into the mind and soul of any young person. This obsession has to be broken in the spirit realm through prayer so the blinders can come off and the afflicted person can see the truth. If it's never completely broken, the person with the disorder can experience it creeping back in his or her mind again and again.

Don't think it can't happen to your grandchildren. This blinding spirit can target anyone. But prayer can stop it before it ever takes hold, as well as bring about the release of someone already held captive by it. It's such a dangerous disorder that medical and psychological help must be sought immediately as well. So if that ever presents itself in one of your grandchildren, pray for the right professional people to help. Thank God for the needed doctors and therapists who can save his or her life. If your grandchildren have shown no sign of this terrible disorder, pray they never will.

Ask God to deliver your grandchildren from every plan of the enemy in their lives.

We all know that sickness or infirmity can hit anyone through no fault of their own. They can be inherited. Because of certain genetics in a family line that people may not be aware of, some diseases might not be able to be prevented. Still, we must pray that God will protect our grandchildren from all sickness, chronic diseases, disorders, infirmities, and weaknesses that run in families. If you know of certain conditions or weaknesses that run in the families of your grandchildren, lay a spiritual ax to the root of that family tree by praying that all formerly inherited diseases or infirmities stop manifesting themselves with your grandchildren.

When your grandchildren do get sick, pray that God will heal them. Pray that they will know God as their Healer and learn to turn to Him as their Lord who heals. The Bible tells how people touched Jesus in some way and they were healed. Pray that your grandchildren learn to touch Jesus in prayer, in praise, and by being in His Word so they can find the healing He has for them.

If you have a grandchild who was born imperfect, I'm sure you are already praying for him or her every day to overcome those disabilities. We have a precious little one like that in our extended family. The grandparents and the parents were heartbroken, of course, but God has been with them every step of the way. They have asked for prayer support from everyone, and countless people have responded. They now have many praying family members and friends who are lifting them up every day of this difficult journey. And we will never stop praying for this beautiful child because God has an important purpose for every life. And we all believe He is the Healer and Restorer, and nothing is impossible for Him.

If that is the situation with one of your grandchildren, don't hesitate to ask for prayer for that child and his or her family from other strong believers. Don't go through this without prayer support. If your prayers are not answered in a way you hoped they would be, and the disability is not reversed as you would like, pray that a cure will be discovered, or there will be new medicine or therapies that will bring great relief and improvement. Don't stop praying for these miracles. It may be that this child was born for such a time as this, so that ongoing prayer will be lifted up for a cure, or that some form of prevention can be discovered.

Many parents and grandparents are going through this, but when they have strong and consistent prayer support from others, they are better able to get through each day. And *you* need that prayer support as well. Don't discount your own pain. Ask people to pray *with* you and *for* you and for the child and the parents. Pray for every possible improvement needed in order to move forward. The Bible says, "We know that all things work together for good to those who love God, to those who are the called according to His purpose" (Romans 8:28). Ask God to show You the good He is bringing forth in each of your lives.

My Prayer to God

Lord, I pray for my grandchildren to have good health all the days of their lives. Protect them from wasting and devastating diseases. Specifically, I pray for (name each grandchild and anything that concerns you about his or her physical health).

You've said in Your Word that "My people are destroyed for lack of knowledge" (Hosea 4:6). Don't let my grandchildren be destroyed because they or their parents lack knowledge about how to take care of their bodies. Give them the desire to eat healthful food. I know that every child left to himself will most likely eat enticing food that can do more harm than good. Give my grandchildren the gift of good sense and a desire for food that will bless their bodies with health. Help them to consider the condition of their health seriously and not take good health for granted. Teach them that they cannot think they will forever get away with doing whatever they want. Help them to turn to You for guidance as to what they *should* do and *should not* do in order to maintain good health.

I pray that my grandchildren will also learn to take care of their bodies with proper exercise and rest. Help them make choices to not allow bad things into their bodies that will harm them, such as drugs, alcohol, cigarette smoke, and junk food. Take away all attraction for anything that will make them sick.

Keep my grandchildren from eating disorders of any kind. Enable each of them to not be swayed by a lying spirit that causes them to sit in judgment upon their body, comparing it to the world's image of "perfection." Help them to love their body and be thankful to You for all it can do instead of criticizing it.

Keep my grandchildren from inheriting any family weakness or infirmity. If there is any disease that is common on either side of their biological families, I lay a spiritual ax to the root of that family tree and pray that this physical or mental tendency stops and does not manifest with this child. Reveal anything that needs to be done in order to prevent that.

Teach my grandchildren that their body is the dwelling of Your Spirit, and they must keep their house for God's Spirit clean. (See 1 Corinthians 6:19-20.) Enable them to realize that they are the caregiver of their body, but You, Jesus, are the Healer, and You can heal them sovereignly or lead them to the medical help they need. Instill in them the knowledge that You "took our infirmities and bore our sicknesses" (Matthew 8:17). Thank You, Jesus, that because of what You accomplished on the cross, we can be healed.

In Jesus' name I pray.

God's Word to Me

If you diligently heed the voice of the LORD your God and
do what is right in His sight,
give ear to His commandments and keep all His statutes,
I will put none of the diseases on you which I have
brought on the Egyptians.
For I am the LORD who heals you.

EXODUS 15:26

Do you not know that your body is the temple of
the Holy Spirit who is in you,
whom you have from God, and you are not your own?
For you were bought at a price;
therefore glorify God in your body and
in your spirit, which are God's.

1 CORINTHIANS 6:19-20

Whether you eat or drink, or whatever you do,
do all to the glory of God.

1 CORINTHIANS 10:31

The prayer of faith will save the sick,
and the Lord will raise him up…
pray for one another, that you may be healed.
The effective, fervent prayer of
a righteous man avails much.

JAMES 5:15-16

12

Lord, Give My Grandchildren Good and Wise Doctors

*T*oo many times in my life I have had certain health problems, and no doctor could figure out at the time what was wrong. About 15 years ago, I was so sick with attacks of pain and nausea that I ended up in three different emergency rooms three separate times over a period of about 10 months, and I saw a number of doctors and specialists, and yet no one could get to the bottom of it. As a result, I nearly died.

Finally, one night around midnight, I felt something explode in my lower abdominal area. The pain was so excruciating I knew I would die from it. I thought my appendix had ruptured, so my husband drove me to the emergency room. I should have let Michael call an ambulance, but I truly thought I would die before they could respond.

When we arrived at the hospital, I could hardly talk, but I told the doctors I thought my appendix had ruptured. For hours they did tests on me but found nothing. I knew I wasn't going to survive if someone didn't do something soon, so I begged every medical person who came into my room to help me. No one did.

My husband, sister, and a close friend were at the hospital with me, praying that God would send someone to save my life. Finally, after nearly eight hours, a doctor came in and bravely decided to do exploratory surgery to find the problem. As it turned out, I was right. My appendix had ruptured, and I had been in agony all those hours with that poison spreading throughout my body. The doctor told me after the operation that if he had waited one more hour to act, it would have been too late. I thanked him every time I saw him after that for saving my life, and I told him he was God's answer to our prayers.

The recovery was long and painful. I asked God, "Why could no other doctor find anything wrong after all the tests and examinations I had been given that night? Why could not one medical professional figure that out?" I felt as if there were blinders on everyone. And no one would listen to my pleading for help.

I have also seen that same kind of situation happen to both of my children. Each child had a medical problem at a different age, and each one experienced a different devastating diagnosis. It wasn't that no one could find something wrong, as it had been with me. Rather, in each case the diagnosis was incorrect. I had no peace about it both times, and I believed with all my heart that it was not the future God had for either of them.

My daughter received a terrible diagnosis when she was about five. I prayed intensely about it and found no peace. I got a second opinion, and although it was different, it was still not acceptable. My husband and I prayed for God's guidance as I checked everywhere I could for help. I finally found it at a wonderful children's hospital in Los Angeles. They had a new, cutting-edge treatment, and they were so positive they could help her with this that after we left there that day, my daughter and I both felt great hope. She went through a few years of their prescribed protocol, and the condition eventually disappeared. If I had accepted the verdict of the first two doctors, she would not be where she is today.

When my son was in his twenties and out of college, he received a devastating diagnosis of a wasting disease. When we prayed about it, I again had no peace in my spirit regarding that judgment. So we prayed and prayed that if this was a mistake, God would reveal it. Or, if it was not a mistake, that He would give us peace that He would heal him or get us through this. As it turned out, another doctor found that my son's symptoms were the result of a terrible reaction to a diet sweetener in a soda he had been drinking far too regularly.

I have heard from a number of other people about that same kind of situation happening to them or their children or grandchildren—where there was either a problem with finding any kind of diagnosis at all, or a wrong diagnosis was given and the person received what amounted to a life sentence with no hope.

It may sound as if I am critical of doctors, but I am absolutely not. Far from it. I am beyond grateful for them, and I thank God for them and for the many times they have saved my life. But even they will tell you they don't know everything. They, too, need prayer. That's why we must pray for our children and grandchildren to have good and wise doctors, and to always be correctly diagnosed. Pray that the enemy cannot put a shroud of mystery over a problem and conceal it from medical professionals.

Parents can easily become totally overwhelmed when a child is sick. They need wisdom to know who the right doctor is for them, as well as perhaps what physical therapists to see and what should be done. Things can happen to children medically that can negatively affect their lives forever. We have to pray they will be led to doctors who are not only gifted to diagnose the problem, but will also protect them from bad drugs and medical errors. We must pray medical professionals will have wisdom and clarity from God as to what the exact right thing is for our grandchildren.

Ask God to protect your grandchildren from ever being misdiagnosed or given the wrong medicine or treatments that could harm them. Pray there will be no mistakes in any of the hospitals or doctors' offices they are in. Pray that any doctor they see will be given divine guidance from God in diagnosing and treating their sickness, disease, or infirmity.

If your grandchild is not yet born, pray for wisdom for the doctors and nurses who will be attending the birth. Pray that nothing goes wrong in the womb, and no problems occur during the delivery or in the time thereafter. Pray always for perfect health and development for your grandchild, and that there will be no mistakes or misjudgments made.

There is a difference between living in denial about something and refusing to accept what you believe in your spirit is not the final judgment on a child's life. Ask God to show you the difference in your grandchildren's lives, and to show their parents as well. Believe that God wants to heal and restore, and ask Him how to pray and what to do. Before accepting a negative verdict on a grandchild, pray and ask God to show you what *His* will is. Ask Him to reveal if the diagnosis is correct, and if so, to give you peace about it. If a troubling diagnosis is correct and God has allowed it, pray that a new treatment will be discovered to help this child improve. Ask God to do miracles in this child's life. Pray for the parents to have strength, health, and faith to trust God to enable them to meet the challenges ahead and make good decisions.

Remember that you know the God for whom nothing is impossible. Pray first and ask God to give you peace about whether to accept what seems to be inevitable or if you are to search for something better.

My Prayer to God

Lord, I lift up my grandchildren to You. (Name each grandchild before God.) I ask that You will provide each of my grandchildren with good, excellent, and wise doctors, nurses, medical technicians, and physical therapists to treat them as needed. Keep them from ever being misdiagnosed or given improper treatment. Give discernment to every doctor they see so that they are never prescribed the wrong drug and given medicine that will do damage to them in any way. If there is ever a misdiagnosis, reveal it right away so that proper treatment can be given. Give all of their doctors the wisdom and good judgment needed to do what is best for them.

I also pray for godly wisdom for my grandchildren and their parents or caretakers so they will know what to do in every situation that requires medical treatment. Don't let them wait too long to get the medical care they need. Give the parents or caretakers the insight to select the right doctor. I pray they will not accept a bad verdict that sentences their children to a hopeless outcome. Give them insight to know when You have something better for them. Help them to ask, seek, and knock until they have found the right doctor and the proper care. Keep us all from accepting the judgment of man as being higher than Your ability to heal. At the same time, don't let us live in denial about something if it is Your will that we walk through it with You.

I pray You will remove a shroud of mystery over any health problem my grandchildren may have. Bring the truth to light for all to see—especially doctors and other medical personnel. You will always know exactly what the problem is and can not only reveal it, but also clarify what needs to be done about it.

Give my grandchildren's parents the means to pay for all necessary medical treatments. Provide insurance and medical aid for them so they can always get help. Give me the means to help in any way I can as well.

Give my grandchildren and their parents a sense of peace when they are seeing the right doctor and the diagnosis is correct. Give them wisdom for every decision they must make.

In Jesus' name I pray.

God's Word to Me

Heal me, O LORD, and I shall be healed;
save me, and I shall be saved, for You are my praise.

JEREMIAH 17:14

"I will restore health to you and
heal you of your wounds," says the LORD.

JEREMIAH 30:17

The things which are impossible with men
are possible with God.

LUKE 18:27

Ask, and it will be given to you; seek, and you will find;
knock, and it will be opened to you.
For everyone who asks receives, and he who seeks finds,
and to him who knocks it will be opened.

MATTHEW 7:7-8

Let him ask in faith, with no doubting,
for he who doubts is
like a wave of the sea driven and tossed by the wind.
For let not that man suppose that
he will receive anything from the Lord.

JAMES 1:6-7

13

Lord, Keep My Grandchildren Far from the Harm of Evil People

*I*n this world and at this time, we absolutely must pray for our grandchildren to be protected from evil people who prey on boys and girls and young men and women. I know this subject is not something we want to even think about, but we must so that we can be praying powerfully and ongoingly about it. We cannot allow ourselves to believe these things could never happen to our children or grandchildren so that no prayer would be needed.

There is an epidemic in our godless society we cannot ignore, and that is pornography. Viewing pornography has become a mental and emotional addiction perpetuated by purveyors of evil and the enemy of God and our soul. Surprisingly, it is even rampant in the church. The statistics revealing the percentage of Christian men—including pastors and church leaders—who are in church and viewing pornography on a regular basis are staggeringly high. It is unimaginable.

Even worse is that many of these men go on to view *child*

pornography. And too many of them act out their viewing addiction on children around them. I cannot imagine how brain damaged, utterly selfish, and spiritually dead a person has to be in order to view precious children as objects to be used for their sexual entertainment. How can anyone sink so low as to care nothing about how much damage is inflicted upon the core of a child's being so that this innocent young person is scarred for life?

I have personally prayed with far too many distraught mothers and grandmothers who told me they discovered their young son, or daughter, or grandchild was being sexually molested and abused by a stepfather, stepgrandfather, uncle, trusted friend, caretaker, someone at camp, church leader, athletic trainer, or, in some cases, even the child's own father. And these perpetrators were thought to be Christians just because they went to church. They obviously were not Christians at all because it is impossible that darkness and light reside together in the same person.

If this problem is that bad *in* the church, how much worse is it *outside* the church? If this is happening among supposed Christians, how bad is it among unbelievers in the rest of society? It is beyond what we think.

Law enforcement and other watch groups have lists of convicted and registered child sex offenders, and you can find out how close they are to your house or the houses where your children and grandchildren live. This is worth checking into because, believe me, nothing will cause you to pray more fervently than to find out how many there are and how close they live. And these are only the ones who have been caught and convicted.

I cannot overemphasize the seriousness of this problem. It

doesn't matter what area you live in. Even in the nicest and seemingly safest communities they are there. Why they are even out of jail is a mystery to me, but registered sex offenders cannot hide because their name, address, and sometimes even a photo of them is available for all to see.

Predators can be lurking anywhere, so pray that anyone who has access to your grandchildren not have evil intentions. As grandparents, we must establish a spiritual wall around our grandchildren, asking God to surround them with His angels so they are protected from evil at all times. We can assume nothing.

Be ruthless in your prayers—not only for your precious grandchildren, but for all vulnerable children in the areas where your grandchildren live and also where you live. Pray that child sexual abusers will be exposed to the light, punished for their crimes, and put away from society.

This sickening cancer of the mind and soul must be stopped. If we don't intercede, who will?

Pray that your grandchildren will always know where the boundaries are with other people. Pray they will not be afraid to tell a trusted parent, grandparent, other family member, or close friend when anyone violates those boundaries and makes them feel uncomfortable. Pray that parents will listen when their children tell them of violations of their physical privacy.

If your grandchild has already been abused in some way, pray that it will all come to light and the proper authorities are notified. Pray that the abuser will be fully revealed, exposed, brought to justice, and forced to pay for what he has done with long-term incarceration and not just a slap on the wrist.

Jesus said that for those who harm a child, it would be better if they were dead. He said, "Whoever causes one of these little ones who believe in Me to stumble, it would be better for him if a millstone were hung around his neck, and he were thrown into the sea" (Mark 9:42). There is an ultimate justice for child sexual abusers that is far worse than anything they will ever receive on this earth, and it lasts for eternity. God does not think kindly of anyone who causes another to sin—especially children.

Jesus was very clear about how much He values children. He said, "Take heed that you do not despise one of these little ones, for I say to you that in heaven their angels always see the face of My Father who is in heaven" (Matthew 18:10). He compared the heart of a child to the way we need to be when we come to receive Him—humble and pure. When He spoke about the lost people who recently came to Him in faith, He compared them to little children whom no one should ever lead astray. He said of them, "It is not the will of your Father who is in heaven that one of these little ones should perish" (Matthew 18:14).

The enemy is not lightening up on his intent to destroy our children and grandchildren, so don't lighten up on your intent to protect them in prayer. Don't listen to the enemy's lies telling you this is too big or scary an issue for you to pray about. That is one of the enemy's greatest deceptions. Your prayers have power because it is *God's* power working through them. Be assured that Jesus is fully on your side as you pray about this. The Bible says, "Do not be overcome by evil, but overcome evil with good" (Romans 12:21).

You do more good than you can imagine when you pray.

So keep praying "lest Satan should take advantage of us; for we are not ignorant of his devices" (2 Corinthians 2:11).

Pray that anyone around your grandchildren who has in his heart to do evil will be exposed for who he is and what he's doing. Anyone who is intent upon doing evil—especially to a child—has bowed his heart to serve Satan. God's Word says that we are to "submit to God. Resist the devil and he will flee from you" (James 4:7). We can resist the enemy—on behalf of our grandchildren—in prayer.

Pray that your grandchildren are never violated by evil people who intend to do them harm.

This is one of the most important prayers you will ever pray for your grandchildren—no matter what age they are.

My Prayer to God

Lord, I lift up my grandchildren to You. (<u>Name each grandchild before God.</u>) I ask that You would protect each of them from all evil people—whether at school, or daycare, or wherever they are—with babysitters, neighbors, camp counselors, family members, coworkers, or friends who have bad intentions toward them. I pray that my grandchildren will never be abused in any way. Deliver them from evil, and reveal any potential abuser *before* anything bad happens. Where evil people lurk, expose their plans.

Give my grandchildren the discernment and wisdom to know when people are not trustworthy. Enable them to sense evil quickly if it comes near them. Help them to immediately identify when someone is doing anything inappropriate. I pray that if anything is done to my grandchildren that is a violation against them, it will be reported to someone in authority in their lives, especially parents and law enforcement. Keep my grandchildren from being intimidated by the threats of those people who want to do them harm.

If any abuse or contact with evil people has already happened, I pray You would bring to light who the perpetrators are. Expose their evil actions in a court of law, and let them be punished for their crimes. Lead the parents of that grandchild to find professional help for their child so that they can fully recover what has been lost and heal whatever has been broken in them as a result.

Surround my grandchildren with Your angels so that no person intending to do evil to them will ever find an opportunity to do so.

In Jesus' name I pray.

God's Word to Me

Deliver us from the evil one.

MATTHEW 6:13

Whoever receives one little child like this
in My name receives Me.

MATTHEW 18:5

The light has come into the world,
and men loved darkness rather than light,
because their deeds were evil.
For everyone practicing evil hates the light
and does not come to the light,
lest his deeds should be exposed.

JOHN 3:19-20

Abhor what is evil. Cling to what is good.

ROMANS 12:9

A good man out of the good treasure of his heart
brings forth good things,
and an evil man out of the evil treasure
brings forth evil things.

MATTHEW 12:35

14

Lord, Let No Weapon Prosper That Is Formed Against My Grandchildren

*T*f you know Jesus as your Savior, then you have an enemy. Even if you don't know the Lord, you *still* have an enemy; it's just that you probably don't recognize him as such. You may even think of him as the angel of light he likes to pretend he is, but if you have received Jesus, then you have God's Spirit in you, so you have all the authority and power you need to identify and resist your enemy.

Your enemy is also *God's* enemy. And he hates you because he hates all people who love, serve, and worship God. That's because our enemy wants to himself be worshipped and will try to defeat every person who will not bow down to him. Therefore, he makes war against us and our children and grandchildren.

Our faith in God and His Word, and the purity of our worship and the power of our prayers, are our greatest weapons against the enemy of our soul.

God wants us to become prayer warriors for our children

and grandchildren so that violence will be kept far away from them as well as ourselves. You can think that your spiritual enemy doesn't exist and you are not at war with anyone, but the truth is—as we can clearly see played out in our world today—you don't have to be at war with someone in order for them to be at war with you.

We must realize that this is a spiritual battle, and we are in God's army. His army is the only one where we can be deployed but don't actually have to go anywhere. That's because the battle is waged in prayer wherever we are. Prayer *is* the actual battle. When we pray, we are defeating the enemy. And we are not alone in this, because God has prayer warriors all over the world praying according to His leading. However, you may be the only one praying with fervency for your children and grandchildren.

Just as *God* has a plan for our life and for the lives of our children and grandchildren, the *enemy* of our soul *also* has a plan for us and the lives of our children and grandchildren. But God has given us a way to take dominion over the enemy and his works of darkness, and it's through prayer and the power of God's Word. God calls all of us who believe in Him to go to battle as prayer warriors for His kingdom.

No matter how hopeless a situation may seem to you, God gives you power in prayer to do something about it. Even when you can't see a way out, God can. The enemy may appear strong to you, but God is *all-powerful.* The enemy is not.

The enemy wants to destroy your children and grandchildren just as he wants to destroy you, but your prayers can put a stop to it. And God has given you power in His Word that you can access by claiming it in faith. God has said to His people who believe in Him and His Word that "*no weapon formed against you shall prosper*" (Isaiah 54:17). Commit those words to memory because you will need to speak them often over your family and especially your grandchildren.

For example, if one of your grandchildren is being bullied—as happened to a grandchild of one of my friends—declare that Scripture over your grandchild in prayer. My prayer partners and I did that, and the bully was exposed and suspended from school. In another instance of a friend's bullied grandchild, the parents were able to take the child out of that school when the school would do absolutely nothing about the situation. When they did that, an opening "suddenly" became available in a good Christian school. The problem stopped and didn't come back.

Prayer works!

All it takes is someone who believes in the power of God to do miracles when we pray. When we understand the power of God's Word, and when we have faith enough to believe God means what He says, we can claim His Word for our lives and the lives of our children and grandchildren.

Being a prayer warrior for our grandchildren doesn't mean that nothing bad will ever happen. But if something does happen, your prayers can help them recover from it and keep them from being destroyed by it. Fight in prayer whatever battle you may face, and watch God come to their defense. Call on God's miracle-working power to protect them. Declare often that no weapon formed against your grandchildren will prosper. Thank God for His Word and that He hears your prayers.

Then put it all in God's hands.

My Prayer to God

Lord, I lift my grandchildren up to You. (Name each grandchild before God.) I see that evil is all around us, and so I pray You will always protect my children and grandchildren from it. Send Your angels to guard them and protect them from any plans of the evil one. Break down any strongholds the enemy tries to erect against them.

Thank You for Your Word that says to Your people who love and serve You that "no weapon formed against you shall prosper" (Isaiah 54:17). I claim for my children and grandchildren that no weapon formed against them will ever succeed. Where something bad has already happened to one of my grandchildren, I pray You will bring restoration to that child and to the entire family so that the enemy will be entirely defeated.

Thank You that Your Word says that we who believe in You have "an everlasting foundation" (Proverbs 10:25). I claim the foundation I have in You, and I stand on Your side in this war between good and evil. Your enemy is also mine, and I choose to do battle against him in prayer as You have required. Thank You that "You have armed me with strength for the battle" (Psalm 18:39).

Help me to take up the sword of the Spirit—Your Word—every day because it is my greatest weapon against the enemy. Enable me to be led by Your Holy Spirit as I pray. Enable me to be an unshakable prayer warrior for my children and grandchildren in whatever way You lead me.

I pray You will bring to nothing any plans of the enemy to harm or destroy my children and grandchildren. I pray that only *Your* plans will succeed in their lives. I ask that Your blessings and protection be so powerfully upon them that the plans of evil will never even come near them.

In Jesus' name I pray.

God's Word to Me

We do not wrestle against flesh and blood,
but against principalities,
against powers,
against the rulers of the darkness of this age,
against spiritual hosts of wickedness
in the heavenly places.

EPHESIANS 6:12

The word of God is living and powerful,
and sharper than any two-edged sword,
piercing even to the division of soul and spirit,
and of joints and marrow,
and is a discerner of the thoughts and intents of the heart.

HEBREWS 4:12

In the world you will have tribulation;
but be of good cheer, I have overcome the world.

JOHN 16:33

When the whirlwind passes by, the wicked is no more,
but the righteous has an everlasting foundation.

PROVERBS 10:25

"No weapon formed against you shall prosper, and every
tongue which rises against you in judgment You shall
condemn. This is the heritage of the servants of the LORD,
and their righteousness is from Me," says the LORD.

ISAIAH 54:17

SECTION THREE

*Praying for Your
Grandchildren's
Spiritual Growth and
Development*

15

Lord, Enable Me to Understand What My Grandchildren Face in This World

We are all uneasy about what is going on in the world and what the future holds. We are especially concerned about all that our grandchildren will face—or are facing now. We know it's far more sinister, evil, and threatening to them than what we dealt with at their age. The entire world is becoming increasingly dangerous, and we must ask God to help us understand how to pray specifically for each of our grandchildren.

The Bible says when we don't know how to pray, the Spirit of God helps us. (See Romans 8:26.) We need His help because only God knows what is ahead. Our grandchildren may face things we haven't even imagined. And we may not even be here for the worst of it. But the effects of our prayers can be felt for the lifetime of our grandchildren.

You may be a young grandparent and have no memory of when prayer was not only *permitted* in public places but also *encouraged.* We were allowed to be Christians without persecution, ridicule, or retribution. We had prayer every morning in school, God and Jesus were talked about among teachers and students, and the thought of being sued because of our faith never entered our mind.

Children in public school today are shut off from the Bible and prayer and any teaching about God, so if it doesn't happen in the home by the parents or grandparents, or in a church, it may not happen at all. That's why we see certain children who appear to live without any conscience, who do things that are unconscionable. They didn't experience consequences for their bad behavior when they were young, so they don't consider consequences when they are older. For that reason, not only do our grandchildren need our covering of prayer more than ever—for as long as we are alive on this earth—but so do their parents. In some situations, you may be the only Jesus your grandchildren see or hear.

If we have some idea of what our grandchildren will face, we'll know better how to pray for them. Here are some ways to pray now:

Pray for insight and wisdom about each grandchild concerning what is to come. When you have that, you can pray in advance of bad things happening. You may not know details, but you can be led by God's Spirit to pray in a way that can keep your grandchildren safe in what could be dangerous circumstances.

Pray that your grandchildren's parents do not die prematurely. Pray they are here to take care of their children until the children can take care of themselves. This is very important because no one can replace a good parent. No one will love the child as much or look out for them as well—except for you, of course. In the case of bad parents—and there are relatively few—pray that those parents will be transformed by having an encounter with the one, true, living, all-powerful God who can change them forever.

Pray that no harm comes to your grandchildren, and especially because of persecution. The persecution of Christians will increase as we get closer to the return of the Lord, so you must ask for God's protection and favor upon your grandchildren

Pray that your grandchildren will never be in the wrong place at the wrong time. Only God knows what is ahead, and only He can guide people away from danger. Ask God to give your grandchildren a heart to follow Him so He can lead them to a place of safety. He is well able to do that. This is a good prayer to pray for all of your loved ones.

Pray that your grandchildren will be lovers of God and not lovers of themselves. The Bible describes how people will become lovers of themselves and not lovers of God and His ways. They will care only about themselves and what they want to have or experience, but they will *not care* about what *God* wants for them and what *His will* is for their lives. Pray that this will never be the case with your grandchildren.

There will be many more specific things that the Spirit of God will lead you to pray about, but this is a good start. When He speaks something to your heart, write it down on the prayer page, anywhere else in this book, or in a separate notebook so you won't forget it. God will speak so many things to your heart that it will be hard to remember everything if it is not written down.

My Prayer to God

Lord, I am very concerned for the future of my grandchildren. (<u>Name each grandchild before God.</u>) I cannot bear the thought of any of the things I see happening in this world happening to them. I can only have peace knowing that You will keep them safe from what is ahead. I pray they will stay close to You and hear Your voice guiding them to walk ever closer to You. I pray they will always go to a great church and feel safe and happy there. Give them great pastors and youth leaders who hear from You, never disobey Your laws and commandments, and never violate their trust.

I pray that each of my grandchildren will marry a godly spouse and stay happily married and raise godly children. I pray You will hide them in Your shadow from the enemy. (See Psalm 17:8-9.)

Show me how to pray for my grandchildren regarding all they will face in their lives. I see evil and danger increasing in this world every day with no indication that it will be getting better. I know Your Word says that wickedness will increase, and people will more and more be lovers of themselves and not lovers of You and Your Word. I pray that my grandchildren *will be lovers of You and Your Word and not lovers of themselves.* Pierce their conscience if they consider choosing another path than the one You have for them.

Give me knowledge about how to pray regarding the specifics of what my grandchildren are facing now or will face in the future. Show me what it will be like in their schools, in their workplaces, in their families, and with their peers. Guide me so I can pray in advance of the things that will happen in the world around them. Only You know the future and all they will face. Only You can keep them safe and help them to accomplish great things for Your kingdom. Just as David knew to pray morning, noon, and night, help me to keep praying like that as well. Keep me from neglecting my grandchildren by ceasing to pray for them. Give me strength, health, and a clear mind until I go to be with You.

Your Word says that in the world we will face problems, but You "have overcome the world" (John 16:33). Thank You that You have done so much for us. Thank You that You have all the answers and all the help we need. Thank You that You are greater than anything I or my grandchildren or their parents will face. Help us turn to You in every situation. Thank You that Your Word says we can have peace in You no matter what tribulation we face.

In Jesus' name I pray.

God's Word to Me

The Spirit also helps in our weaknesses.
For we do not know what we should pray for as we ought,
but the Spirit Himself makes intercession for us
with groanings which cannot be uttered.

ROMANS 8:26

Evening and morning and at noon I will pray,
and cry aloud,
and He shall hear my voice.

PSALM 55:17

I pray for them. I do not pray for the world
but for those whom You have given Me, for they are Yours.

JOHN 17:9

Pray without ceasing.

1 THESSALONIANS 5:17

As for me, I will see Your face in righteousness;
I shall be satisfied when I awake in Your likeness.

PSALM 17:15

16

Lord, Lead My Grandchildren's Parents into a Close Relationship with You

*P*arents don't know how to raise a child in the ways of God if they don't know what God's ways are. And children not raised according to God's ways can bring sorrow to their parents. Any parent who turns his or her back on God and His Word can bring undesirable results in his or her children.

Our actions have consequences for our children and grandchildren. People have suffered because of the sins of their parents and grandparents. We see horrible things happening in certain places in the world because of sin in the land for which no one has repented. The same sin and hatred is carried on and on from generation to generation, passed down like an inheritance. And no one tries to put an end to it because they are either ignorant of how it can be done, or they are blinded by evil, or they are willfully ignoring the truth of God about it.

The prophet Jeremiah told the people what God said would become of them—and their children—because they did not live His way. God foretold that when Jeremiah showed the people the words of this prophesy, they would ask, "'*What is our sin that we have committed against the* LORD *our God?*' then you shall say to them, '*Because your fathers have forsaken Me,*' *says the* LORD; 'they have walked after other gods and have served them and worshiped them, and have forsaken Me *and not kept My law. And you have done worse than your fathers, for behold, each one follows the dictates of his own evil heart, so that no one listens to Me.* Therefore I will cast you out of this land into a land that you do not know…*where I will not show you favor*'" (Jeremiah 16:10-13).

And that is exactly what happened.

God sees all sin. But He has given us a way out of the consequences of sin. And that is at the feet of Jesus in prayers of confession and repentance. We can always come to Him to be free of the consequences of sin even if it was committed by someone else in our family. There are not only consequences for parents when they don't live God's way, but those consequences also affect their children. That is why we must pray for our grandchildren's parents to have a close relationship with God.

We are all much better off when we get rid of whatever causes us to sin. Jesus said clearly, "If your eye causes you to sin, pluck it out and cast it from you. It is better for you to enter into life with one eye, rather than having two eyes, to be cast into hell fire" (Matthew 18:9).

I know that can sound harsh, but it's the truth.

We have to get rid of anything in our lives that perpetuates sin—or the consequences of it—on our children or grandchildren. We do that in prayer. We can say, "Lord, show me anything in *me* that I need to be free of, and I will ask for forgiveness from You to clear the slate. For I do not want anything to be inherited by my grandchildren because of sins of their parents or grandparents. Show me anything in my family line that has been an abomination to You, and I will confess it to You on behalf of my family."

Pray that your grandchildren's parents will be convicted in their consciences of any sin in their lives so they will bring it before God and be free. It's not our place to be the Holy Spirit to them, so we must be careful to not drop "subtle hints" or get in their face about anything unless we know for certain we are being led by God to do so. At least, not if we ever want to see our grandchildren again. Our prayers will accomplish far more than our words anyway. And if we *do* need to speak to our grandchildren's parents, praying first will give us a heart of love for them, and our words will have more penetrating power. If the parents ask you for anything resembling *advice,* you can lovingly give that to them and suggest how much a close relationship with God can benefit the whole family.

No criticism. Just unconditional love.

Your grandchildren need godly parents raising them, so pray that the parents of your grandchildren will have a *loving* and *committed relationship* with the Lord. God shows kindness and favor to those who love and serve Him. If there is a parent whose heart is turned against God, pray that his or her heart will be broken before God and remolded to be like the Lord's heart of love.

David was a man after God's own heart because he had a *repentant heart.* His sins were great—not the least of which were committing adultery, murder, lies, and not disciplining his own children. And there were consequences for those sins that affected his children severely. We don't want our grandchildren paying for their parents' mistakes. We need to pray for their parents to live lives submitted to God and obedient to His ways. This is crucial for their future well-being and their spiritual growth. If a parent has a heart that is hard against God and His ways, pray that God will do whatever it takes to penetrate the hardness and wake up that person to the truth.

Although the Bible says the sins of the parents are visited on the children to the third and fourth generation, it also says when the parents return to the Lord, the children are blessed. However, even if a parent never comes to the Lord, at a certain age the children themselves are accountable to God. They can make a decision to receive Jesus and live His way, and when they do, they will be blessed in spite of what their parents have done. The good news is that your grandchildren who receive Jesus can break the influence of sin in their family heritage by living for God and standing on His Word in their lives.

If any one of the parents of your grandchildren does not know Jesus, do not stop praying for him or her until that parent does.

No matter where your grandchildren's parents are in their walk with God, you can always pray they will be led into a *closer* walk with Him. We've heard of way too many godly people—sadly, even pastors—who have been led astray by the sins, lures, and lasciviousness of this world. Godly people need our prayers too so they will not be blinded and led astray by the enemy of their soul to their destruction.

Pray that your own relationship with the parents of your grandchildren will always be close and full of love and respect. That is extremely important for your grandchildren to see, because it helps form their own understanding of *God's* love.

My Prayer to God

Lord, I pray that each of my grandchildren's parents will be drawn into a deep and committed relationship with You. (Specifically name the parents, stepparents, or guardians of each of your grandchildren.) I see in Your Word that children and grandchildren have a great advantage if their parents instruct them how to live Your way and then show them by serving You. Help these parents to fully understand Your ways and Your love, and communicate them to their children.

Bring godly people into the parents' lives to guide them in Your way. Lead them to a good, vibrant, Bible-believing church so that they and their children will be fed by Your Spirit and not the spirit of the world. Open doors to small Bible studies and prayer groups so godly friendships can grow out of them. Give them eyes to see when they are not living Your way. Convict them if at any time they are not living the kind of life You want them to model for their children.

Give my grandchildren's parents a love for Your Word. Bring it alive to them so that the words leap off the page and into their heart to stay. No matter where they are in their walk with You, bring them closer. If any of them does not know You, draw that person to receive You as his or her Savior. If they do profess to know You, bring them into a greater knowledge of who You are and what Your Word says. Cause them to be a godly influence in their children's lives. Give the parents wisdom in raising their children so that they impart to them a desire to live Your way.

Show me anything in me or my past that has not been brought to You in repentance, and I will confess it before You as sin. I want to be set free of anything negative that could be visited upon my children or grandchildren. I pray also that any parent's wrong actions will be repented of so that no consequences for them will come near his or her children. Remove all family sin that could affect the parents' or grandchildren's lives.

In Jesus' name I pray.

God's Word to Me

I have no greater joy
than to hear that my children walk in truth.

3 John 4

A foolish son is a grief to his father,
and bitterness to her who bore him.

Proverbs 17:25

Children's children are the crown of old men,
and the glory of children is their father.

Proverbs 17:6

If your hand or foot causes you to sin,
cut it off and cast it from you.
It is better for you to enter into life lame or maimed,
rather than having two hands or two feet,
to be cast into the everlasting fire.

Matthew 18:8

My eyes are on all their ways;
they are not hidden from My face,
nor is their iniquity hidden from My eyes.

Jeremiah 16:17

17

Lord, Draw My
Grandchildren to Know
You Better Every Day

A child who knows God—a child who has Jesus in his or her heart—becomes a person who knows *who* God made him or her to be. Praying for our grandchildren to have a solid and close relationship with God is easier if the parents know Him too, of course. But even if they don't *yet* know Him, we can pray that our grandchildren learn to love God and receive Jesus as their Savior. Depending on the situation, we as the grandparents may not have a lot of influence over that, but we have power through our prayers to pray that our grandchildren will have hearts that are open to the Lord.

Pray that God will pour out His Spirit on your grandchildren and make Himself known to them in undeniable ways.

There is a great sense of security you feel about your children and grandchildren when you know that they have a strong relationship with the Lord. If their heart is open to Him, He can speak to them and help them to live out His will. But we must continue to pray that they are drawing closer to Him every day and not straying off the path He has for them. I have seen the heartbreak of parents who raised godly children, only to see them go off to college or out in the world and then become godless unbelievers. We do not want that for our grandchildren.

Ask God to show you what you can do as far as communicating how wonderful it is to walk with Jesus and rely on His Word. Ask God what the best way is to communicate *His love* to them. All the little gifts and books you give them, the help you offer to them, the letters you send them—messages of encouragement and love—add up over time. The love of God in you for them comes across loudly. Of course, you always have to be sensitive to the wishes of the parents, but you don't have to become someone you are *not* in order to do that. If the parents are not believers and you are, ask God to *use you* to *show Him* to them in ways that will communicate His love. Always being there for them with unconditional love breaks down many barriers—especially if you pray in advance for that to happen.

Pray that the Word of God will come alive to your grandchildren and take root in their heart, so that even the simplest verse becomes life for their soul.

You have the great advantage of knowing how horrible life can be without God. So ask Him to show you how you can share that with your grandchildren at the right time and in an age-appropriate way. If you are able to spare them any of the misery that happened to you because you didn't know God at the time—or didn't follow His ways—ask God to show you what that would be. Your own testimony is a powerful tool to encourage another person's salvation. It makes life in the Lord real to a person who does not have that reality now.

My own children married spouses whose families were all strong believers, something for which I am grateful every day. I had prayed for that specifically for more than three decades before they met the person they married, but it's never too late to start praying about that. If your children did not marry believers, and whose parents and grandparents are not believers, your prayers for them can change all that too. You can be the prayer warrior on their behalf that brings them to the Lord.

The power of a praying grandmother or grandfather is formidable in the spirit realm. That's why we must pray for our grandchildren every day. And not only the ones who are here now, but also those who may come in the future even after we have gone to be with the Lord.

God made a promise to Israel, saying, "*I will put My law in their minds, and write it on their hearts; and I will be their God, and they shall be My people.* No more shall every man teach his neighbor, and every man his brother, saying, 'Know the LORD,' for they all shall know Me, from the least of them to the greatest of them, says the LORD. For I will forgive their iniquity, and their sin I will remember no more*" (Jeremiah 31:33-34).

Pray that God will engrave His Word on the heart of each of your grandchildren. Pray that He will draw your grandchildren toward Him every day by giving them a desire to know Him and experience all He has for them.

Praying is one of the best ways we get to know God. And prayer is one of the ways our grandchildren will establish their close relationship with Him too. Because it's never too early to teach a child to pray, praying should be a part of their lives as soon as possible. Teach them to pray for God's blessing on their meals and to pray in the morning for their day. Show them how to pray for people and situations throughout the day, and teach them to pray at night before they go to bed, thanking God for their day and His protection. My children have never known life without praying to God being part of it. I see them teaching their children to pray early too. I love that. It gives me great peace.

This is definitely worth praying about for your grandchildren.

My Prayer to God

Lord, draw my grandchildren close to You. (Name each grandchild before God.) Help them to come to know You in a deep and committed way so that their relationship with You grows every day. Teach them to understand Your laws and commandments, and help them keep Your ways faithfully. Enable them to be so strong in Your Word that they inspire their own parents and friends. Show my grandchildren's parents and me how to communicate Your Word to them in ways they understand and retain so that they are always drawn to it.

I pray You will put Your laws in the mind and heart of each of my precious grandchildren so that they will make decisions to live Your way. Give each one a heart that wants to draw near to You so that You will draw near to them. Show them that the world can never answer to their deepest longings. Help them to see that their greatest priority in life is to love You with all their heart, soul, mind, and strength. (See Mark 12:30.) And in doing that, You will supply all their needs.

Show me everything I can do to teach my grandchildren about who You are and all You've done. Show me the examples in my own life, or the life of someone I have known, that make a powerful point about the dangers of not knowing You and not living Your way. Most of all, Lord, help me to communicate Your love to them in ways they can fully comprehend.

Teach my grandchildren to be praying people. Help me to pray with them every opportunity I have. Teach their parents to pray with them too so that they grow to know the fulfillment of communicating with You. Teach them to call upon You for everything. Guide them on the path You have for them. Give them a desire to grow closer to You every day and follow You all the days of their lives.

In Jesus' name I pray.

God's Word to Me

Draw near to God and He will draw near to you.

JAMES 4:8

The name of the LORD is a strong tower;
the righteous run to it and are safe.

PROVERBS 18:10

The LORD is near to all who call upon Him,
to all who call upon Him in truth.

PSALM 145:18

On the last day, that great day of the feast,
Jesus stood and cried out, saying,
"If anyone thirsts, let him come to Me and drink."

JOHN 7:37

Repent therefore and be converted,
that your sins may be blotted out,
so that times of refreshing may come
from the presence of the Lord.

ACTS 3:19

18

Lord, Teach My Grandchildren to Resist Rebellion in Themselves

*G*od does not bring forth children for trouble. He promises that we who serve Him, and teach our children to do the same, will all be blessed. *"They shall not labor in vain, nor bring forth children for trouble; for they shall be the descendants of the blessed of the LORD, and their offspring with them"* (Isaiah 65:23).

As a parent or grandparent, we must often remind ourselves of this Scripture.

When a child seems to often cause trouble, or bring trouble upon his family, it is a work of the enemy. That is, unless you can see it is directly influenced by the rebelliousness of one or both of the parents, in which case you must pray for a spirit of rebellion to be broken over the parents as well as your grandchild.

I am not talking about very young children who have not yet learned the right thing to do. I am talking about children who know better and yet choose to be rebellious against their parents or authorities in their lives.

The enemy wants our grandchildren on his side, and he will tempt them to be rebellious against their parents. Our enemy first rebelled against God, and he wants our children and grandchildren to do the same. So children will test their limits with their parents until it is proven to them in all certainty where the boundaries are. Pray that the parents of each of your grandchildren will be able to discern when a rebellious spirit is rising up in their child and that they will know how to stop it.

Correcting a child breaks a yoke of rebellion. Whenever a child does not have proper correction, it sends him closer to the hands of the enemy. The Bible says, "Do not withhold correction from a child" (Proverbs 23:13-14). The last half of that verse talks about beating the child with a stick. This doesn't mean a child has to be beaten in the way we know the meaning of that word today. That is unthinkable. It means his punishment must be felt. It could mean removing his favorite possessions or restricting his activities until he repents and chooses to be obedient. If a parent waits too long to correct a child, he or she will fail to send a message that there are consequences for bad behavior. The child may not get that message before something terrible happens to him or to someone else because of him. If a child does not *feel* correction in some way, their rebellion will only intensify.

If *parents won't* discipline their child for having a rebellious spirit, the *enemy will*. (See Proverbs 17:11.)

The Bible also says, "My son, do not despise the chastening of the LORD, nor detest His correction; *for whom the LORD*

loves He corrects, just as a father the son in whom he delights"
(Proverbs 3:11-12).

With all that being said, parents need wisdom about what
correction works for each child. Every child is different. It
took a lot to convince our son that obeying us and resisting
all thoughts of rebellion were good moves for him. With our
daughter, it usually only took a stern look of disapproval to see
immediate repentance in her heart. The Bible says, "Chasten
your son while there is hope, and do not set your heart on his
destruction" (Proverbs 19:18).

That says it all.

Every child is known by his deeds—by whether he does the
right thing or has a rebellious attitude. A child gets a reputa-
tion when people make judgments about him—whether other
kids like him or not, and whether other adults with godly stan-
dards want to even be around him. As a common practice, we
should pray often that each of our grandchildren will have a
heart that listens to instruction. "Cease listening to instruction, my son, and you will stray from the words of knowledge"
(Proverbs 19:27).

The root of all rebellion is pride.

The Bible says we should not be prideful or rebellious, but
rather we should come to God as little children. Jesus said,
"Unless you are converted and become as little children, you
will by no means enter the kingdom of heaven. Therefore, *whoever humbles himself as this little child is the greatest in the kingdom of heaven*" (Matthew 18:3-4). That means we must pray
that our grandchildren will be humble and teachable—and not

prideful or arrogant—for this is the only way they can enter God's kingdom on earth as well as in eternity.

Ask God to show you what is going on in the heart of each grandchild so you can pray that a spirit of rebellion is never permitted to establish a stronghold.

Pride is what Lucifer allowed in himself when he was God's worship leader in heaven. His pride caused him to become enthralled by his own beauty, and he rebelled against God. You may wonder why God didn't discipline him. But He *did*. Lucifer was cast out from heaven and became Satan, a created being with no good future and no hope. Jesus said, "I saw Satan fall like lightning from heaven" (Luke 10:18). Jesus wasn't just envisioning this; He was there in heaven when it happened. Jesus gave His life so that we could have victory over death and hell and *"over all the power of the enemy"* (Luke 10:19).

Ask God to give your grandchildren a repentant heart. A repentant heart has no rebellion in it. It's quick to feel the pain of sinful thoughts, attitudes, and actions and repents right away before God. A person with a repentant heart is swift to say, "Forgive me" to God, to parents, to whomever he or she has offended. This will serve him or her well all the days of their lives.

My Prayer to God

Lord, I lift up my grandchildren to You. (<u>Name each grandchild before God.</u>) I ask that they will grow up without arrogance and pride. Cause each one to have a humble heart and a teachable spirit. Help them learn to be humbly submitted to You as well as to their parents and legitimate authority figures in their lives.

I pray no rebellious thoughts would be allowed to take root in their mind or heart. Keep them from any rebellion against You or their parents. Enable their parents to recognize a rebellious attitude immediately and have the wisdom to do what it takes to put a stop to it. Give them sharp discernment so they do not allow it to grow in their children and become established. Enable me to recognize it in my grandchildren as well and resist it mightily in prayer and in communication with that child. Take away any rebellious spirit, and give each grandchild a humble heart of reverence for You.

Thank You, Lord, that my children and grandchildren were not brought forth for trouble (Isaiah 65:23). Where one of my grandchildren has brought trouble upon himself or herself or the family, I pray You would bring deliverance to that child's heart. Break down any alignment with the enemy. Destroy any desire to be *associated* with rebellious people or to *idolize* people who are rooted in rebellion. Free that child to be used powerfully for Your purpose and not the enemy's.

If any of my grandchildren have a strong will,

teach them to submit their will to You and not to their own desires. Help that strong-willed child to instead become a strong leader in Your kingdom who is dependent on You. Cause them to be a force for good and not evil. Enlighten them to recognize any rebellion in themselves and totally resist it. Give them a pure heart, and take away all desire to dominate or control other people. Give the parents wisdom to not be controlled by their child. Give each of my grandchildren a heart that wants to serve You and others according to Your leading and Your will in his or her life.

In Jesus' name I pray.

God's Word to Me

He who is often rebuked, and hardens his neck,
will suddenly be destroyed, and that without remedy.

PROVERBS 29:1

He who begets a scoffer does so to his sorrow,
and the father of a fool has no joy.

PROVERBS 17:21

Hear, my son, and be wise;
and guide your heart in the way.

PROVERBS 23:19

An evil man seeks only rebellion;
therefore a cruel messenger will be sent against him.

PROVERBS 17:11

He brings out those who are bound into prosperity;
but the rebellious dwell in a dry land.

PSALM 68:6

19

Lord, Keep My Grandchildren from Straying into Enemy Territory

We don't need to have a sinful or rebellious spirit in order to stray into enemy territory. It can happen by just being careless or ignorant with regard to traps of the enemy to destroy us.

Being tempted is not a sin. Not walking away from temptation is.

The enemy is always planning evil and destruction, and the only thing that restrains him are the prayers of the prayer warriors. Our prayers can help keep the enemy from finding an opening into our grandchildren's hearts.

You are a prayer warrior or you wouldn't be reading this book. God wants to use you to keep the enemy far from your children and grandchildren. Remember that you are not *going into* the enemy's territory when you pray. You are *taking back territory* the enemy has stolen. If you see your grandchild stepping into enemy-controlled territory, claim that child for God's kingdom. "Resist the devil" on that child's behalf, and the devil "will flee from you" and that grandchild. (See James 4:7.)

Your prayers on behalf of your grandchildren have power because they have the power and will of God behind them. There is no greater power than that.

It is through your prayers that God's power is directed. He set it up that way. That's why He wants you to partner with Him in prayer.

When Simon Peter was being attacked by Satan, Jesus prayed that he would *have strong faith to stand against it.* Jesus said, "Simon, Simon! Indeed, Satan has asked for you, that he may sift you as wheat. *But I have prayed for you, that your faith should not fail"* (Luke 22:31-32). Jesus had to pray that His disciple—who was with Him every day—would have strong faith to resist the enemy. How much more should we pray for our grandchildren to have faith to resist the enemy when they are tempted to be led astray by him?

Jesus said to His disciples, *"Pray that you may not enter into temptation"* (Luke 22:40). How much more should we pray that same prayer not only for ourselves, but also for our children and grandchildren? Pray that they will be kept far from the hands of the enemy. Pray that they will have *the fear of the Lord* and *not the fear of man*, because "The fear of man brings a snare, but *whoever trusts in the LORD shall be safe"* (Proverbs 29:25).

A snare is a plan set up by the enemy for our demise. But our faith in God gives us a place of safety from it.

If Your Grandchild Has Already Strayed

If your grandchildren are older and have already strayed off the path God has for them, pray that God will do whatever it takes to get them back on it. A person can stray into enemy territory because of attraction to the world's way of thinking. Also being drawn to sin of any kind without repentance before God, or parents, is a trap.

For those grandchildren who have already stumbled into enemy territory, pray they will come to the Lord and be attracted to His ways. Pray that God will lead them back from the land of the enemy. The promises of God to His people about their children are,

> Refrain your voice from weeping, and your eyes from tears; for your work shall be rewarded, says the LORD, and *they shall come back from the land of the enemy* (Jeremiah 31:16).

> Lift up your eyes all around, and see: They all gather together, *they come to you;* your sons shall come from afar, and your daughters shall be nursed at your side. *Then you shall see and become radiant, and your heart shall swell with joy* (Isaiah 60:4-5).

We all rejoice when we see our children and grandchildren return to the Lord.

Every time you think about your straying grandchild, recite the following verse: *"There is hope in your future, says the LORD, that your children shall come back to their own border"* (Jeremiah 31:17).

Claim that verse for your straying grandchild and pray accordingly.

Your hard labor in prayer will result in your grandchildren coming back from the enemy's territory. No matter how far they have strayed from the life God has for them, He will bring them back to where they are supposed to be.

Because God's promises are not an entitlement program we automatically get, He requires us to pray.

We must consistently praise God that He will bring our children back to the way they were raised when they were brought up in His ways. I have seen the heartbreak of grandmothers when the answer to their prayers is delayed regarding grandchildren who have strayed into enemy territory. If that is you, I encourage you to trust that God sees your tears and hears your prayers. The delay may be because He is dealing with a strong will in that child. When your heart weeps before the Lord for your grandchildren, you can rejoice in knowing that something was accomplished in the spirit realm that will manifest itself in the physical as well.

The truth is, "*He who continually goes forth weeping, bearing seed for sowing, shall doubtless come again with rejoicing,* bringing his sheaves with him" (Psalm 126:6). Thank God that one day you will rejoice over the fruit of your prayers, which are sown as seeds in the lives of your grandchildren.

Jesus spoke a parable suggesting that people *always ought to pray and not lose heart* (see Luke 18:1). So keep that in mind and don't let yourself fall into deep discouragement about your children or grandchildren when they don't respond quickly to your prayers. Continue praying.

Remember that "our light affliction, which is but for a moment, is working for us a far more exceeding and eternal weight of glory, while we do not look at the things which are seen, but at the things which are not seen. For the things which are seen are temporary, but the things which are not seen are eternal" (2 Corinthians 4:17-18).

Don't lose heart. If we are praying, things are happening. It's just that we cannot see what is happening—yet.

The Bible says, "All things work together for good to those who love God, to those who are the called according to His purpose" (Romans 8:28). But in the two verses before that it talks about praying and how the Holy Spirit helps us to pray according to God's will (Romans 8:26-27). Can it be, then, that things work out for good when we are praying? I believe so.

The truth is that "the eyes of the LORD run to and fro throughout the whole earth, *to show Himself strong on behalf of those whose heart is loyal to Him*" (2 Chronicles 16:9). God looks for people who love Him and pray fervently so He can move powerfully on their behalf. If we have a heart that is loyal to God, the Bible says, "*In all these things we are more than conquerors through Him who loved us*" (Romans 8:37).

Resist the enemy by not giving up on praying for your grandchildren, no matter what happens. If the enemy turns up the intensity on your children or grandchildren, then you turn up the fervency of your prayers.

My Prayer to God

Lord, I lift my grandchildren before You. (Name each grandchild before God.) I know in Your Word You promised Your people that if they would serve You, You would bring their children back from the lands of the enemy and cause them to return to You. Because I love You and want to serve You all the days of my life, I believe this promise is for me too. I pray that if any of my children and grandchildren stray into enemy territory, You would bring them back to You.

Jesus, You prayed for Your disciples that God would "keep them from the evil one" (John 17:15). I pray the same for my grandchildren—that *You would keep them from the evil one.* Where they have already strayed into enemy territory, I pray that You would bring them back. I pray they will follow You all the days of their lives and not turn from Your ways.

Keep my grandchildren from being blinded by the enemy's lies. Teach them to always see Your truth. Enable them to hear Your voice leading them, and silence the voice of the enemy. I pray they would understand the spiritual battle we all face and all You have done for those who resist the lure of the enemy. Give my grandchildren discernment so they can clearly differentiate between good and evil. Enable them to be strong enough to not "give place to the devil" (Ephesians 4:27). Strengthen them to "abstain from every form of evil" (1 Thessalonians 5:22).

Whenever the enemy turns up the intensity of his attack on my grandchildren to lead them into his territory, help me to increase the fervency of my own prayers against him, knowing that I am on Your side and doing Your will.

In Jesus' name I pray.

God's Word to Me

Be sober, be vigilant; because your adversary the devil
walks about like a roaring lion,
seeking whom he may devour.
Resist him, steadfast in the faith,
knowing that the same sufferings
are experienced by your brotherhood in the world.

1 Peter 5:8-9

Test all things; hold fast what is good.
Abstain from every form of evil.

1 Thessalonians 5:21-22

I will contend with him who contends with you,
and I will save your children.

Isaiah 49:25

"God resists the proud, but gives grace to the humble."
Therefore submit to God.
Resist the devil and he will flee from you.

James 4:6-7

Watch, stand fast in the faith, be brave, be strong.

1 Corinthians 16:13

20

Lord, Cause My Grandchildren to Be Attracted to Godly Friends

*W*e have all seen how the entrance of one ungodly friend into a child's life can influence him or her in a negative way. It doesn't necessarily mean that the friend is a bad person, but perhaps the two of them together do not produce good results. That's why, no matter what age our grandchildren are, we must pray for them to have good, godly, obedient, believing friends. The Bible says that we are not to be "yoked together with unbelievers" (2 Corinthians 6:14). That doesn't mean our grandchildren can never be around friends who do not believe in God. It means that their closest friends—the ones who have the most influence in their lives—should be believers.

We can always pray for any unbelieving friends to come to know the Lord, but that often doesn't happen quickly, if at all. And we don't want to wait too long to test the waters with regard to our grandchildren.

Pray for your grandchildren's parents to have clear discernment about this. Sometimes they are so overwhelmed by their lives that they are just grateful their children *have* friends at all and don't take time to vet them with the Lord. Only God truly knows who is a bad influence on your grandchildren and who is not. And the truth regarding that may not be the way it first appears. In other words, the person who seems to be a good friend may actually bring about negative results when he or she gets together with your grandchild.

I know a precious praying grandmother who asked me to pray for her grandson. She had always been very close to him since birth because she often took care of him as he was growing up. She said he was a delightful child, and there was a deep bond of love and affection between them. They did many things together and had great fun, and she always took him to church with her when he was in her care. He was obedient and smart and showed great promise for his future success.

Unfortunately, when he became a teenager, he got involved with some bad friends. They did ungodly things, and at 18 he ended up in jail for stealing. She now constantly prays for him while he is in prison, and her heart grieves for him. We have prayed together that God will reach him while he is incarcerated. We asked God to send people to speak the truth about God's love for him. We prayed that he will have a clear revelation of how much he needs to turn his life over to God and gain a clear vision of what *he can be*. We asked that God would give him an unshakable desire to do things differently. We also prayed that when he gets out of prison, all the old connections to bad friends will be broken—that his bad friends either be transformed or moved out of his life.

Another praying grandmother I know prayed for her grandchild, who was incarcerated, that the fear of God would be instilled in him in an unforgettable way, and that he would give up the friends who led him to end up in jail in the first place. Her prayers were answered in a major way when the young man ended up in a holding cell of an overcrowded jail with about 15 other criminals. The experience frightened him so much that he vowed he would never allow himself to be in that terrible position again. He received a true vision from God of how he was born for greater things. He left his old friends completely and worked hard to go to college. To this day he has held a good job and has never gotten in trouble again.

A praying grandmother can be a formidable barrier to a life of criminal activity with ungodly friends.

A great church is often the best place to meet godly friends. Pray that your grandchildren's parents will take them to church so they can meet good friends from godly families. If the parents don't take their children to church, see if they will let *you* do that if they live close enough for you to do so. If taking your grandchildren to church is not possible for you, pray that some other caring person will volunteer to do that. I have a friend who takes her five grandchildren (ranging from age two to sixteen) to church with her nearly every weekend—and they love it because the church has a fantastic department for every age. The hardworking parents of these children are very happy she does that because they get to sleep in on that day, and they know this church is something each child looks forward to. Pray that your grandchildren will find godly friends wherever they are and be attracted to that kind of person. Pray they have *discernment* to know when a friend is not godly, and the *strength* to be able to resist that individual's influence in their life.

My Prayer to God

Lord, I lift up my grandchildren to You. (<u>Name each grandchild before God.</u>) I ask that You will bring godly friends into each of their lives. I know how the wrong friends can lead them away from You and Your ways. Please keep that from happening with my grandchildren. Your Word says a great deal about the benefits of godly friends, so Your warning is clear. Lead them to good schools and good churches where godly friends can be found.

Take away from my grandchildren any attraction in them toward friends who will cause them to stray away from the path You have for them. Disturb their conscience so badly that they will refuse to seek the acceptance of people who will draw them away from You and Your ways. Give them a clear vision of the consequences of spending time with ungodly friends that could lead to their destruction. Cause them to refuse to go down that path.

Where friends who are a bad influence have already entered their life, cause my grandchildren to pull away from them. Make their parents well aware of it. Give me revelation about it as well, and show me how to intercede for them. Break up those friendships and remove any bad influence from their life. Do not allow the plans of evil to succeed in any one of my grandchildren through the influence of ungodly friends.

In Jesus' name I pray.

God's Word to Me

The righteous should choose his friends carefully,
for the way of the wicked leads them astray.

PROVERBS 12:26

Do not be unequally yoked together with unbelievers.
For what fellowship has righteousness with lawlessness?
And what communion has light with darkness?...
Or what part has a believer with an unbeliever?

2 CORINTHIANS 6:14-15

Do not enter the path of the wicked,
and do not walk in the way of evil.

PROVERBS 4:14

Can two walk together, unless they are agreed?

AMOS 3:3

He who walks with wise men will be wise,
but the companion of fools will be destroyed.

PROVERBS 13:20

21

Lord, Give My Grandchildren Godly Wisdom and Understanding

We all want our grandchildren—as well as our children—to have the kind of wisdom that comes from God. That is *true* wisdom. Without it they cannot make proper decisions, discern good from evil, or be able to understand the true character of another person.

The Bible says that wisdom begins when we have deep reverence for God. (See Proverbs 9:10.) God pours His wisdom—the Spirit of wisdom—into the heart of the person who reverences Him. Having wisdom given by the Holy Spirit to your grandchildren will give them innate understanding that will serve them well all of their lives.

The Bible says, "A wise son makes a glad father, but a foolish son is the grief of his mother" (Proverbs 10:1). It pleases parents when their children are wise and not foolish. "My son, if your heart is wise, my heart will rejoice" (Proverbs 23:15).

On the other hand, "a child left to himself brings shame to his mother" (Proverbs 29:15). This is talking about a child who is not corrected. Without correction they have no wisdom and will make foolish choices. They become prideful. "A man's pride will bring him low, but the humble in spirit will retain honor" (Proverbs 29:23).

A child can be spared from so many terrible things just by having the wisdom to make right decisions. With all the evil and deception out in the world, they cannot navigate successfully through life without it. They need discernment in order to not trust the wrong people. Godly wisdom enables them to hear when God is speaking to their heart, telling them which way to go.

God's Word says, *"Happy is the man who finds wisdom, and the man who gains understanding; for her proceeds are better than the profits of silver, and her gain than fine gold. She is more precious than rubies, and all the things you may desire cannot compare with her. Length of days is in her right hand, in her left hand riches and honor. Her ways are ways of pleasantness, and all her paths are peace. She is a tree of life to those who take hold of her, and happy are all who retain her"* (Proverbs 3:13-18).

That means wisdom is more valuable than all the greatest treasures on earth, because it brings a long, pleasant, peaceful, and happy life.

Money can't buy that.

Godly wisdom is far beyond education and knowledge about things. It's a constant sense of the truth that allows people to make right decisions. They can figure out the details of their life far more successfully if they have the Spirit of wisdom guiding them.

The Bible says, "A wise man will hear and increase learning, and *a man of understanding will attain wise counsel"* (Proverbs 1:5). A heart that is humble and willing to listen to the advice of godly people will bring blessings upon that person. The Bible says God calls us to seek the Spirit of wisdom, and He will pour wisdom into us. But when we reject His counsel, He is not pleased. *"Because you disdained all my counsel,* and would have none of my rebuke, *I also will laugh at your calamity;* I will mock when your terror comes" (Proverbs 1:25-26). All we have to do is simply ask God for wisdom and He gives it to us. And we can ask for it not only for ourselves, but also on behalf of our children and grandchildren. And we can pray that they will come to understand the value of asking God for it themselves.

The opposite of a wise person is a foolish one. There are enough warnings in the Bible about being a fool that it stirs us on to pray much about that.

Those who reject knowledge are fools. "Fools hate knowledge" (Proverbs 1:22). But when fools start listening to God, He rewards them with wisdom and understanding. *"Turn at my rebuke; surely I will pour out my spirit on you*; I will make my words known to you" (Proverbs 1:23).

When people reject the opportunity to have wisdom, they will come to regret it. *"Then they will call on me, but I will not answer; they will seek me diligently, but they will not find me. Because they hated knowledge* and *did not choose the fear of the* LORD, *they would have none of my counsel* and *despised my every rebuke.* Therefore they shall eat the fruit of their own way, and be filled to the full with their own fancies. For the turning away of the simple will slay them, and the *complacency of fools will destroy them"* (Proverbs 1:28-32).

That is a scary warning, and we do not want any of that for our grandchildren.

Godly wisdom gives us insight, sound judgment, and a strong sense about the right things to do. We want our grandchildren to always know what the right thing is to do in every situation.

Godly wisdom gives us common sense. Godless people don't have that. People with no common sense are unable to see the full consequences of their actions before they act.

I know I don't have to convince you about the need for wisdom in your grandchildren. We all have made stupid mistakes in our lives and wish we would have had God's wisdom in us at the time. We've all lived long enough to know the value of wisdom from God and would like to spare our grandchildren from the terrible things that can happen to people who have no common sense.

That's why we need to pray.

My Prayer to God

Lord, I pray You will pour out Your Spirit of wisdom upon my grandchildren. (Name each grandchild before God.) Your Word says, "If you *cry out for discernment, and lift up your voice for understanding,* if you seek her as silver, and *search for her as for hidden treasures;* then *you will understand the fear of the LORD, and find the knowledge of God*" (Proverbs 2:3-5). I cry out for discernment on my grandchildren's behalf. Give them a desire for godly understanding. Cause them to seek You for wisdom. I know from Your Word that wisdom comes through Your Holy Spirit.

Keep them from doing foolish things so that they don't have to suffer the consequences that await every fool. Give them wisdom to walk away from danger and evil. Help them hear Your voice telling them which way to go (Isaiah 30:21). Make my grandchildren wise enough to discern between what is clean and what is not. Give them the wisdom they need to determine the true character of the people around them so they don't allow evil people into their lives. Teach them to listen to "wise counsel" (Proverbs 1:5).

Your Word says that "the ear that hears the rebukes of life will abide among the wise" (Proverbs 15:31). "He who disdains instruction despises his own soul, but he who heeds rebuke gets understanding" (Proverbs 15:32). "The fear of the LORD is the instruction of wisdom, and before honor is humility" (Proverbs 15:33).

For my grandchildren I ask as Paul did that "you may be filled with the knowledge of His will in all wisdom and spiritual understanding," and that "you may walk worthy of the Lord, fully pleasing Him, being fruitful in every good work and increasing in the knowledge of God" (Colossians 1:9-10). I pray that You, Lord, will deliver my grandchildren from the powerful darkness of ignorance and carry them into Your "kingdom of the Son of [Your] love" (Colossians 1:13).

In Jesus' name I pray.

God's Word to Me

The fear of the LORD is the beginning of wisdom,
and the knowledge of the Holy One is understanding.

PROVERBS 9:10

The father of the righteous will greatly rejoice,
and he who begets a wise child will delight in him.

PROVERBS 23:24

When wisdom enters your heart, and knowledge is
pleasant to your soul,
discretion will preserve you; understanding will keep you,
to deliver you from the way of evil,
from the man who speaks perverse things.

PROVERBS 2:10-12

A fool vents all his feelings,
but a wise man holds them back.

PROVERBS 29:11

Whoever loves wisdom makes his father rejoice,
but a companion of harlots wastes his wealth.

PROVERBS 29:3

Praying for Your Grandchildren's Provision and Well-Being

22

Lord, Help Me to Be a Godly Role Model for My Grandchildren

We don't live in a vacuum. Everything we do—or *don't* do—can affect our family in some way in the spirit realm. For example, God's Word says, "Blessed is the man who fears the LORD, who delights greatly in His commandments. *His descendants will be mighty on earth*" (Psalm 112:1-2). That means that even though each person is responsible before God for their own relationship and walk with Him, there are still countless blessings and benefits for our children and grandchildren because we love, serve, worship, honor, and obey God.

What a magnificent promise from God to His people who reverence Him and live His way. That's why, no matter how long and how well we have walked with God, it's always good for us to humbly ask that He show us if there is anything in our heart or in our life that does not please Him. After all, any one of us can have unforgiveness, bitterness, doubt, or unloving thoughts toward someone and not think of it as sin. Those attitudes often creep in without us even realizing it if we don't ask God to help us stay aware. It's better to get all sin out in the open before God so we can confess it to Him and be free of any hindrance to our prayers being answered.

Because our descendants receive blessings when we live God's way, it's important that we not only always live God's way, but that we demonstrate it in real ways that are clear to them.

Showing Our Grandchildren God's Ways

One of the things God wants us to do is tell our children and grandchildren about Him—what *He* has done on earth as well as in our personal lives, and what He is doing *in* us at the present time. These truths are supposed to be passed down. *"Let your children tell their children, and their children another generation"* (Joel 1:3). God doesn't want all of the great things He has done for us to be kept a secret from our grandchildren. *"We will not hide them from their children, telling to the generation to come the praises of the* LORD, *and His strength and His wonderful works that He has done"* (Psalm 78:4).

We can share with our grandchildren how blessed people are who love Him and live His way. We can tell the stories of our lives, or of people we know, who lived God's way and were blessed—or who *didn't* live God's way and paid the consequences. We are to love God enough to never forget about all the things He has done, so that "the generation to come might know them, the children who would be born, that they may arise and declare them to their children, that they may set their hope in God, and not forget the works of God, but keep His commandments" (Psalm 78:6-7).

Love what God has taught you, spoken to you, or done for you enough to share it with your grandchildren in age-appropriate ways they can understand.

It's extremely important that we teach our grandchildren about God and the benefits of living His way so that they will tell *their* children who will be born.

When we share God's Word—as well as the specific words the Lord has spoken to our heart—we can impart to our grandchildren a spiritual legacy that will stay with them forever. We can ask God to help us find special nuggets in His Word that would be simple and perfect to communicate to our grandchildren when we see them, write to them, or talk to them. If we don't do it like a sermonette, but rather in a natural sharing and joyfully caring manner, it will penetrate their heart—especially if we pray first for that to happen.

God wants His Word to be passed down from generation to generation, but we can't think that it is going to happen automatically no matter what we do or don't do. It doesn't work that way. We have to not only be in the Word, but also let the Word be in *us*. We must let the Spirit of God bring it alive in *our* heart so that it overflows from us to our grandchildren and speaks to them through us. And we must *pray* for that to happen.

The truth is, everything we have secured in the Lord and learned from God can be lost in the next generation. We have all seen that happen in families far too often. The enemy of every believer will constantly try to steal away everything that is of God from us—including our children and grandchildren. But we have the power in prayer to stop it. It's *God's power*, and He works powerfully through *our prayers*. But we must not *only* pray. God also says we must *tell*.

Unless we tell the things we know of God to the next genera-
tion, and pray for them to retain that in their heart, we can't just
assume our grandchildren will grow up knowing and loving Him.

Building Up What Has Been Broken Down

It may be that some relationships have broken down in your
family. If so, don't blame yourself for that, and don't blame
others, either. It's a waste of time and accomplishes nothing. A
breach in family relationships is a plan of the enemy. He hates
families because they are part of God's plan for us, so he devises
ways to steal ours. Forgive yourself and others and get to the
business of a prayer warrior—praying.

If you ever feel hopeless or despairing about the broken relationships in your family, I want you to understand the power
of what is promised in Isaiah 58 about what happens when we
fast and pray. God describes the kind of fast *He* wants, which
is to break down strongholds, "to *loose the bonds of wicked-*
ness, to *undo the heavy burdens,* to *let the oppressed go free,* and
that you *break every yoke"* (Isaiah 58:6). And so much more,
as if that were not enough. Then He describes all that will be
accomplished because of a fast, such as healing, deliverance,
answered prayer, guidance, strength, ceaseless refreshing, restoration, and more.

What family doesn't need all that?

God says fasting with prayer is one of the best ways to see
powerful breakthrough in your life and your family. He said,
"Those from among you shall *build the old waste places*; you
shall *raise up the foundations of many generations*; and *you shall*
be called the Repairer of the Breach, the Restorer of Streets to
Dwell In" (Isaiah 58:12).

If you see waste places and crumbling foundations in your family, for whatever reason, know that God works miracles when you fast and pray. That's because it's His will to have your family not only stay intact, but be established solidly on the rock of Jesus Christ and His Word. By fasting and praying, *you* can be "the Repairer of the Breach" who helps to build up the foundation of the family again.

The following great promise to those of us who love and serve God is the reason we can never stop praying. "As for Me," says the LORD, "this is My covenant with them: My Spirit who is upon you, and *My words which I have put in your mouth, shall not depart from your mouth, nor from the mouth of your descendants, nor from the mouth of your descendants' descendants,*" says the LORD, "from this time and forevermore" (Isaiah 59:21).

The Bible says, "The righteous man walks in his integrity; his children are blessed after him" (Proverbs 20:7). Pray that the truth of this Scripture will be clearly evident in you and your family.

Someday, one of the things I want to share about the Lord with my grandchildren—when they are old enough to understand—is about God's promise of heaven and being with Him forever. I want to tell them that because I am much older than they are, one day I may get sick or very tired and God will take me to heaven to be with Him. But I don't want them to feel sad about that—well, maybe at first, because hopefully I will have been a blessing to them, but not forever. That's because I will be very happy in heaven. Even though I will miss them, I will be joyful to be with Jesus. I won't be sick anymore. I will have a beautiful mansion to live in and wonderful food to eat, and everyone there will love God and one another. There will be nothing to be afraid of because there is no pain or sorrow there. And one day, when it is time for *them* to go be with the Lord, Jesus will also meet them. And I will be there to greet them as well. And we will be together with the Lord and our loved ones forever in the most beautiful and wonderful place we can ever imagine.

I will tell them that God always has good things ahead for those who love Him.

My Prayer to God

Lord, I lift up my grandchildren to You. (<u>Name each grandchild before God.</u>) Help me to be a godly and great role model for them. Etch Your Word in my heart so deeply that I not only understand it and retain it, but it will become so much a part of me that it overflows to my children and grandchildren in the way I live and talk. Show me how to impart Your Word to each of my grandchildren in lovely and edifying ways so that it becomes part of them and is engraved on their heart as well. Enable me to always speak it as a blessing they love to hear and not a judgment that turns their heart off to it.

Show me any sin in my life that I need to confess before You. I don't want anything to interfere with Your promises to pour blessings on my descendants because of the righteous life I live before You. Help me to live a long and healthy life so I can be a positive, loving, and active influence on my grandchildren. I pray the same for their parents. Your Word says that the "children of Your servants will continue, and their descendants will be established before You" (Psalm 102:28). I pray that for my family.

I pray that each one of my grandchildren—even those not yet born—will serve You all the days of their lives. Keep them from ever being snatched out of Your hands. Help me to lay such a foundation for them in Your Word and in prayer that even after I have gone to be with You, the foundation of Your Word will serve them well. Enable me to share Your Word in such an inspiring way that it will be passed down from generation to generation.

Enable me to always "continue earnestly in prayer, being vigilant in it with thanksgiving" (Colossians 4:2). I pray also that You would open to me "a door for the word, to speak the mystery of Christ" to my children and grandchildren (Colossians 4:3). Teach me to always give good advice whenever it is sought. If I feel strongly that I must *offer* godly advice that is not sought, enable me to discern Your will in the manner I am to do it.

Thank You that the good I do for You not only blesses *You*, but it also blesses my *children* and *grandchildren* and those descendants yet to come as well. Let my life be a testimony of the greatness of living Your way and keeping Your commandments. Make me to be like a sweet-smelling fragrance to my grandchildren because of the beauty of Your love and life in me.

In Jesus' name I pray.

God's Word to Me

Take heed to yourself, and diligently keep yourself,
lest you forget the things your eyes have seen,
and lest they depart from your heart
all the days of your life.
And teach them to your children and your grandchildren.

DEUTERONOMY 4:9

Though they join forces,
the wicked will not go unpunished;
but the posterity of the righteous will be delivered.

PROVERBS 11:21

Their descendants shall be known among the Gentiles,
and their offspring among the people.
All who see them shall acknowledge them,
that they are the posterity whom the LORD has blessed.

ISAIAH 61:9

O my God, do not take me away in the midst of my days;
Your years are throughout all generations.

PSALM 102:24

The LORD God is a sun and shield;
the LORD will give grace and glory;
no good thing will He withhold
from those who walk uprightly.

PSALM 84:11

23

Lord, Give the Parents of My Grandchildren the Ability to Provide Well for Their Family

One of the many great blessings God gives us when we live His way is His provision.

King David said, "I have been young, and now am old; yet *I have not seen the righteous forsaken, nor his descendants begging bread*" (Psalm 37:25). When we are merciful and generous, our "descendants are blessed" (Psalm 37:26). God "does not forsake His saints; they are preserved forever, but the descendants of the wicked shall be cut off" (Psalm 37:28).

God's promise for those who reverence, love, and obey Him is that He will provide for them. "*The generation of the upright will be blessed.* Wealth and riches will be in his house" (Psalm 112:2-3). This is not a guarantee of being wealthy in money and belongings. That is up to God's will. But we can have wealth in many ways, such as good health, plenty of food, clothes that serve their purpose, a place of safety to live, and things that don't break down.

God promises to provide for us, but He doesn't drop groceries from the ceiling. Often He provides by opening doors of opportunity to good work and enabling us to do it. So we must pray for the ability of our grandchildren's parents to be able to take care of the needs of their children.

First of all, ask God to show the parents of your grandchildren what they should be doing in their work and how they can best support their family. Ask God to bless the work they do and to give them a sense of balance in how hard they work. God's Word says, "*Do not overwork to be rich*; because of your own understanding, cease! Will you set your eyes on that which is not? For riches certainly make themselves wings; they fly away like an eagle toward heaven" (Proverbs 23:4-5).

Pray that the parents will not be workaholics who sacrifice their children's well-being on the altar of seeking riches that disappear instead of making their children their main priority.

This is a very important focus for your prayers. As a child, my mother and father lived paycheck to paycheck, and too often one paycheck didn't extend to the next because they were few and far between. Because of that, I often went to bed hungry as a child, which was frightening. And they could only afford one cheap pair of shoes for me each year. This meant that I would outgrow them and they would fall apart halfway through the year. The soles fell off and had to be reglued by my father. But they still kept coming off—sometimes at school or on my way walking to school—and could not be glued. One time my mother put rubber bands around the shoes to keep the soles on, and I had to go to school like that. It was mortifying. Everyone noticed them and laughed.

Our home was a run-down shack behind a gas station. Rats ran across my bed at night. No one else in the area had such a terrible place to live. So I could never have anyone come over and see it. Poverty is painful and not fun. People who say they were poor but never noticed it were not living in poverty. It meant they had only one television when their friends had two. Believe me, going to bed hungry and having shoes that have fallen apart with no way to repair or replace them is something you painfully notice.

We don't want poverty and painful struggles for our children or grandchildren. We want God's provision for them. Nor do we want so much wealth for them that they lose sight of their priorities and feel they don't need God. We don't want them to be lazy and not work, nor do we want them to sacrifice everything—including their marriage and their children—going after riches. We want their work to be rewarded and for them to succeed so they can provide their family with what they need.

Pray that God will bless the work of your grandchildren's parents so they can always provide for the needs of their children. And pray that they all will know where their help comes from.

My Prayer to God

Lord, I lift up my grandchildren's parents to You. (Name each parent before God.) I pray these parents will always have good work and that their work will be blessed with success and financial rewards. Protect them from poverty, but also keep them from the kind of wealth that could draw their hearts away from You. Help them to understand that *You* are their provider so that they are always thankful to You for all You have given them, but they must still work diligently to do what You have called them to do. I pray they will seek *You* for provision in their lives and also give back to You and to others as You lead them.

Enable my grandchildren's parents to do their work well so that they find favor with You and others. Help them to be "not lagging in diligence, fervent in spirit, serving the Lord" (Romans 12:11). I pray they will love their work and do the work they love. Don't allow them to ever neglect their children by working so hard that it occupies too much of their time. May they never sacrifice their children on the altar of their careers and cause their children to suffer because of it. Keep them from poverty that injures and wealth that corrupts.

Give my grandchildren's parents a good work ethic that keeps them diligent to do well, but wise enough to avoid the pitfalls of laziness and irresponsibility. Your Word says, "He who has a slack hand becomes poor, but the hand of the diligent makes rich" (Proverbs 10:4). Help them to understand that "so are the ways of everyone who is greedy for gain; it takes away the life of its owners" (Proverbs 1:19).

Where they are lacking in skills, help them to become more educated so they keep growing and improving in order to provide what people need. Open doors of opportunity for them to advance. Close doors they should not walk through. You have said in Your Word that it is a gift from You to be able to enjoy our work (Ecclesiastes 3:13). I pray that my grandchildren's parents will do good work they enjoy. Help them understand that "in all labor there is profit, but idle chatter leads only to poverty" (Proverbs 14:23). Teach them to actually *do* the job and not just *talk* about doing it. I ask that You will "establish the work" of their hands (Psalm 90:17).

Thank You that Your Word says, "The blessing of the LORD makes one rich, and He adds no sorrow with it" (Proverbs 10:22). Let that verse be an inspiration to their hearts to always commit their work to You and ask You to bless it. Show them that their help is in Your name (Psalm 124:8).

In Jesus' name I pray.

God's Word to Me

Who is the man that fears the LORD?
Him shall He teach in the way He chooses.
He himself shall dwell in prosperity,
and his descendants shall inherit the earth.

PSALM 25:12-13

Blessed is every one who fears the LORD,
who walks in His ways.
When you eat the labor of your hands,
you shall be happy,
and it shall be well with you.

PSALM 128:1-2

The labor of the righteous leads to life,
the wages of the wicked to sin.

PROVERBS 10:16

So are the ways of everyone who is greedy for gain;
it takes away the life of its owners.

PROVERBS 1:19

Beloved, I pray that you may prosper in all things
and be in health, just as your soul prospers.

3 JOHN 2

24

Lord, Enable My Grandchildren to Understand Who You Made Them to Be

*O*ne of the most important aspects of a child's well-being is having a sense of who God made him or her to be. And that happens as the child grows to understand who *God is*, and that he or she is *His child*. When children know they belong to God and He is their heavenly Father, it helps them see who *they* are in relation to *Him*.

God said to His people, "'*I will pour My Spirit on your descendants, and My blessing on your offspring'* ...One will say, '*I am the* LORD's' ...another will write with his hand, '*The Lord's*'" (Isaiah 44:3,5). In other words, they will know who *they* are because they know who *God* is, and that they belong to Him.

When people know who God made them to be, that knowledge gives them a sense of purpose. And that sense of God-given purpose keeps them from wasting their life pursuing things that are meaningless. They may not know the details of the purpose God has for them, but that will be revealed to them once they receive Jesus and walk with Him and seek Him for that revelation. When they are very young, it can be enough to simply know that God *has* a great *purpose* for their life, so they won't follow after anyone or anything trying to lead them to stray away from God.

God gives us His Spirit so we can know Him and understand all He has given us—including our purpose. (See 1 Corinthians 2:12.)

When children don't know who they are or who God made them to be, they can easily get off the path God has for them. Or never get on it in the first place. That's when they may follow after anything. They can become insecure, frustrated, anxious, unhappy, or depressed. They try to *make* their life happen, and when it doesn't go the way they think it should—in other words, they don't find the fulfillment, admiration, and success they are seeking—they become critical of themselves. They compare themselves to others and feel like a failure when they think they don't measure up.

When children or young people have a clear sense of who they are, they don't throw their lives away on something insignificant, at best, or damaging, at worst. They don't look to the world to validate them. They look to the Lord.

Young people who are confused about who they are, and what their purpose is, need our prayers. We can pray that God will bring clarity to them because confusion is never from Him. We must pray that God's voice to them will not be drowned out by the world's noise, but that they will clearly hear His voice to their heart, leading them in the right direction.

We all need to know that "In Him also we have *obtained an inheritance*, being predestined *according to the purpose of Him* who works all things according to the counsel of His will" (Ephesians 1:11). Part of the inheritance we have from God is that high purpose He has given us in order to do His will. Understanding that helps us to pray for our grandchildren to be given a clear vision from God about *who He is and who He made them to be*. And we can encourage them in whatever way God shows us about this.

If you have grandchildren who have grown up without any sense of purpose, ask God to give them a vision now for their life so they won't live aimlessly. It's dangerous for a child to have no sense of purpose. The ones who take drugs, commit crimes, destroy people and property, and accomplish nothing good have no sense of godly purpose. If you are praying for one of your grandchildren about this, don't give up. Sometimes it takes a while in a young person who has learned bad habits of thought.

Some children, who are entrenched in an ungodly lifestyle, can take longer than others to figure it out. But on the other hand, God can bring amazing breakthrough when we pray. I have seen it happen. One day an aimless, directionless, wandering child I know woke up with a vision for his life that could have only come from God. And he went full speed ahead to pursue what God had revealed to him. It was miraculous. And it happened in response to the prayers of his parents, grandparents, and family friends.

So don't stop praying for your grandchildren about this until that happens.

My Prayer to God

Lord, I lift up my grandchildren to You. (Name each grandchild before God.) Enable each one to understand who You made them to be. Reveal to them the knowledge of who *You* are so they can understand who *they* are in relation to You. Help each grandchild to know that You are their heavenly Father and they are Your child. And as such, they have an inheritance from You. Give them a clear vision for their life and a sense of why they are here. Teach them to clearly understand that they were created for a purpose. Help them understand what that purpose is.

Help each of my grandchildren to walk with such a sense of Your purpose for their lives that it keeps them from being distracted by worldly pursuits that are meaningless. Take away all confusion about who they are and cause them to hear Your voice to their heart telling them which way to go. Keep them far from worldly distractions that are a hindrance to all You have for them. Don't allow anything to pull them away from Your plans for their lives. Give them each a vision that allows a glimpse of all You have for them, so that they move through life with a sense of Your purpose for them.

Pour out Your Spirit on my grandchildren as You have spoken of in Your Word. Help them to say in their heart, "I am the Lord's" (Isaiah 44:5). Give their parents and grandparents the wisdom and knowledge they need to help them understand that they were born for a high purpose. And even if they don't yet know exactly what that is, as they seek You and walk with You, I know You will reveal it. Show me how to encourage them about this in any way I can.

In Jesus' name I pray.

God's Word to Me

All your children shall be taught by the LORD,
and great shall be the peace of your children.

ISAIAH 54:13

May He grant you according to your heart's desire,
and fulfill all your purpose.

PSALM 20:4

"Let not the wise man glory in his wisdom,
let not the mighty man glory in his might,
nor let the rich man glory in his riches;
but let him who glories glory in this,
that he understands and knows Me, that I am the LORD,
exercising lovingkindness, judgment,
and righteousness in the earth.
For in these I delight," says the LORD.

JEREMIAH 9:23-24

Arise, shine; for your light has come!
And the glory of the LORD is risen upon you.

ISAIAH 60:1

Now we have received, not the spirit of the world,
but the Spirit who is from God,
that we might know the things
that have been freely given to us by God.

1 CORINTHIANS 2:12

25

Lord, Reveal to My Grandchildren Their Gifts and Calling

*J*ust as God has a purpose for the life of each of His children, He has also given each one special gifts and talents to achieve and fulfill that purpose. He will speak to each person's heart about what He has specifically called them to do with their gifts and talents. When we walk closely with God and seek direction from Him for our lives, He helps us to come to an understanding about what our gifts and talents are and how they are to be used.

The Bible says that God "has saved us and *called us with a holy calling*, not according to our works, but *according to His own purpose and grace* which was given to us in Christ Jesus before time began" (2 Timothy 1:9). So our gifts and talents don't determine our calling. Our calling is determined by God, and He enables us to fulfill it with the gifts and talents He has put in us.

Anytime grandparents tell me they feel as though they don't have a purpose anymore, I tell them, "If you have grandchildren, you have a purpose. And God will use every gift and talent you have to fulfill this special calling. I am not saying that is your only purpose, but do not say you don't have one." If you ever feel that way, please know that the very reason I have written this book is to help you fulfill your calling as a prayer warrior for Christ on behalf of this next generation, who need your prayers so desperately.

God knows the call He has on each of your grandchildren. He sees the gifts and talents He has put in them in order to achieve that. We may not yet see them, but He does, and He will reveal them to us as we seek Him for that knowledge.

Pray that your grandchildren will be able to identify early on the gifts and talents God has put in them. Pray for their parents to be able to recognize these as well. Ask God to enable the parents to hear from Him about how to best guide their children in the development and nurturing of those gifts and talents. Their children need to be taught that "*each one has his own gift from God*" so that they are not tempted to covet another's gift (1 Corinthians 7:7).

Pray that your grandchildren will understand that their gifts and talents come from God so that they are thankful to their Creator, who put these gifts in them. Celebrating *Him* rather than celebrating their gifts and talents is a spiritually healthy way to achieve more with those gifts and talents than they could ever do on their own. That's because praising God for their gifts and calling opens the door of their heart so God can pour more of Himself into them. That, along with dedicating their gifts to the Lord, enables them to accomplish great things that will last for eternity.

People who have no idea what God has called them to do, or who cannot identify their gifts and talents, may end up wandering around, wasting their life, and never moving into the plans God has for them. Paul said, "As God has distributed to each one, *as the Lord has called each one, so let him walk*" (1 Corinthians 7:17). We don't want our grandchildren pursuing something out of God's will and apart from what He has called them to do. We don't want them striving after something God is never going to bless.

Ask God to show you specifically about each child, especially when they have numerous gifts and talents. For example, just because someone has a musical gift and talent doesn't mean they are supposed to be in the music business. It *may* be, but not necessarily. God can use their gifts for His glory in many different ways. That's why they need to know exactly what God is calling them to do, and how He wants to use their gifts and talents to fulfill that purpose.

It's important that other people also affirm your grandchildren in the areas where they excel or have the potential to excel one day. Pray for encouragers, affirmers, and godly mentors to come into their lives. Someone, such as an aunt, uncle, teacher, coach, or another praying grandparent, can be especially helpful. Always pray that the gifts and talents in your grandchildren will be used for God's glory and not their own. Pray that they will never strive to be someone or something that they are not. Ask God to give them balance so that they do not become self-absorbed, self-focused, or prideful about their gifts and talents. Pray that they will want God to be in charge of opening doors of opportunity to serve *Him*. If their focus is on Him, He will raise them up.

My Prayer to God

Lord, I lift up my grandchildren to You. (<u>Name each grandchild before God.</u>) Thank You that You have put in each one of them special gifts and talents that are to be used for Your plans and purposes. I pray that You will enable them to live their lives with a distinctive sense of Your calling so they don't become sidetracked away from Your plans for their life. Give each one of them the ability to identify the gifts and talents You have put in them. Teach them how You want those gifts to be dedicated to You and used for Your glory. Reveal it to their parents as well so they know how to nurture and develop those gifts and talents. Reveal it to me, too, so I know how to pray and to encourage them.

Enable my grandchildren to hear the call You have on each of their lives. Use them to make a positive difference in the lives of others. Help me to encourage them in whatever You have called them to do. I pray they will turn to You for guidance and clarity. I ask that You, "the Father of glory," will give to my grandchildren the "spirit of wisdom and revelation" so they can understand Your calling on their lives (Ephesians 1:17).

Help them to "walk worthy of the calling" with which they are called (Ephesians 4:1). Keep them from wasting time going after things that are not Your will for them. Keep them from spending their life trying to figure out what their gifts and talents are and what Your calling is on their life. Speak to them as soon as they will listen and teach them to use their gifts according to Your will.

Send the right teachers, tutors, and mentors to teach and encourage them. Open the mind, eyes, and ears of each child to help him or her clearly see, hear, and understand what You want him or her to do. Whatever any of my grandchildren are struggling with when it comes to learning, I know there is nothing You cannot work out in their lives. Help them see that their struggle doesn't mean failure. Rather, it often accomplishes in them exactly what is needed for them to succeed.

Teach me to always be an encouragement to my grandchildren. Enable me to help them understand that You not only have a calling on their lives, but You will equip them to accomplish it as they depend on You.

In Jesus' name I pray.

God's Word to Me

The gifts and the calling of God are irrevocable.
ROMANS 11:29

Be even more diligent to make your call and election sure,
for if you do these things you will never stumble.
2 PETER 1:10

Whom He predestined, these He also called;
whom He called, these He also justified;
and whom He justified, these He also glorified.
ROMANS 8:30

Having then gifts differing according to the grace
that is given to us, let us use them.
ROMANS 12:6

I, therefore, the prisoner of the Lord,
beseech you to walk worthy of the calling
with which you were called,
with all lowliness and gentleness,
with longsuffering, bearing with one another in love,
endeavoring to keep the unity of the Spirit
in the bond of peace.
EPHESIANS 4:1-3

26

Lord, Keep Each Grandchild's Heart from Turning Toward the World's Idols

*I*dolatry is exalting anything other than God.

The world is filled with idolatry. God blinds the eyes of people who worship idols so that they are unable to see the truth. The Bible says that God "has shut their eyes, so that they cannot see, and their hearts, so that they cannot understand" (Isaiah 44:18). But God never forsakes those who do not forsake Him. (See 1 Samuel 12:22.) It is the ministry of the Holy Spirit to draw hearts back to Himself when they begin to stray—if we ask Him to do so.

The Bible says to "keep oneself unspotted from the world" (James 1:27). It also says that if we strive to be a friend of the world, we become an enemy of God. We definitely don't want to become God's enemy. And we don't want our grandchildren to either.

This is why we must pray that our grandchildren will always have reverence for God and never forget "what great things He has done" (1 Samuel 12:24).

Where children have already gone after the world's idols and brought destruction on themselves, God can redeem those situations. If that has happened to your grandchildren, pray they will be brought to repentance before God. The good news is that even when they make bad choices, there is still a blessing for them when they turn around and follow God. They may have to pay for their transgressions, but not forever. So don't stop praying for them to be brought back to the Lord.

God said of His people who worshipped idols, "*They have turned their back to Me, and not their face.* But in the time of their trouble they will say, 'Arise and save us'" (Jeremiah 2:27). People turn their back on God and go after the world's idols, and then when they get into trouble, they ask God to save them. But God says, "*Where are your gods* that you have made for yourselves? Let *them* arise, *if they can save you in the time of your trouble*" (Jeremiah 2:28).

The people were seeking sorcerers and worshipping other gods instead of seeking the one true God. So after they left *Him*, He left *them*. But in His mercy He said, "Return to Me, and I will return to you," but the people asked God, "In what way shall we return?" (Malachi 3:7). They didn't even see that they had made wealth their idol.

In answer to their question, God told them they had robbed Him by not giving to Him what He has asked them to give. He instructed them to "'*bring all the tithes into the storehouse,* that there may be food in My house, and *try Me now in this,*' says the LORD of hosts, '*if I will not open for you the windows of heaven and pour out for you such blessing that there will not be room enough to receive it.* And *I will rebuke the devourer for your sakes*'" (Malachi 3:10-11).

Pray that your grandchildren do not make an idol out of wealth. Jesus didn't say that we could never have anything, but what we have, or what we *want* to have, should never come between God and us. It should not be first above God in our heart. This is a crucial principle that our children and grandchildren must learn. *When we give to God, He opens heaven and pours out such blessings upon us that we overflow with them.* And He rebukes the devourer of our lives and blesses what we produce.

A person who learns to give to God will always be blessed by God.

The Bible says, "*You shall not go after other gods*, the gods of the peoples who are all around you (for the LORD your God is a jealous God among you), *lest the anger of the LORD your God be aroused against you* and destroy you from the face of the earth" (Deuteronomy 6:14-15).

God also said, "*Nor shall you bring an abomination into your house, lest you be doomed to destruction like it.* You shall utterly detest it and utterly abhor it, for it is an accursed thing" (Deuteronomy 7:26).

We don't want our children or grandchildren to ever go after other gods, nor do we want them to bring anything detestable—such as something that exalts other gods—into their homes because that can open the door to evil in their lives. The Bible says, "He who is joined to the Lord is one spirit with Him" (1 Corinthians 6:17). Pray that they will identify anything in their lives that threatens the unity of Spirit they have with God.

God said to *separate ourselves from people who worship idols and have ungodly practices.* (See Ezra 10:11.) God doesn't change. He is the same today as He was in the past and will be for all eternity. He meant it then, and He means it now and also in the future. The only thing that changes is the shape of the idols. Today, people make idols out of fame, music, money, possessions, other people, or whatever draws them away from God and brings them under the influence of God's enemy.

It's not that any of these things are bad in themselves. The question is, what spirit is behind them? Behind every idol is a spirit of the enemy—a spirit of lust, greed, pride, destruction, deception, and much more. The truth is, "we know that we are of God, and *the whole world lies under the sway of the wicked one*" (1 John 5:19). So if we are walking closely with God, we will know right away what spirit is behind something, or someone, or some place, because God's Spirit gives us that discernment. We can feel the "sway of the wicked one."

Pray for that kind of discernment in your grandchildren. They must be able to discern the difference between the Spirit of God and the spirit of the world—which is from God's enemy. This will be an important distinction they must make for the rest of their lives.

My Prayer to God

Lord, I lift up my grandchildren to You. (<u>Name each grandchild before God.</u>) Show them how to live in this world without being drawn into its darkness. Help them to separate themselves from anything that is detestable to You. Give them the strength to be led by Your Spirit and not influenced by the godless spirit in the world. Help them to reject all idols and stay separate from the traps of the enemy luring them away from all You have for them.

Your Word instructs us, "*Come out from among them and be separate*, says the Lord. Do not touch what is unclean, and I will receive you. I will be a Father to you, and you shall be My sons and daughters, says the Lord Almighty" (2 Corinthians 6:17-18). Help my grandchildren to always remember that they are Your children. Give them a desire to be a friend of Yours and the discernment to never want to be "an enemy of God" (James 4:4).

Keep them from pride so they stay undeceived. Reveal to them quickly whenever they give in to certain obsessions of the culture that are against Your ways. Don't let them bring detestable things into their homes. Keep them from any person or practice that will hinder their prayers from being heard and limit them from receiving everything You have in store for them. Protect them from anything that will ultimately separate them from You and Your best in their life.

"Far be it from me that I should sin against" You,

Lord, "in ceasing to pray for" my grandchildren (1 Samuel 12:23). I pray they will learn to reverence You with all their heart, and to always consider what great things You have done for them (1 Samuel 12:24). I pray they will always worship You and never walk away from You to serve other gods.

In Jesus' name I pray.

God's Word to Me

Do not be conformed to this world,
but be transformed by the renewing of your mind,
that you may prove what is that good and acceptable
and perfect will of God.

ROMANS 12:2

Do not love the world or the things in the world.
If anyone loves the world,
the love of the Father is not in him.

1 JOHN 2:15

Little children, keep yourselves from idols.

1 JOHN 5:21

You are of God, little children, and have overcome them,
because He who is in you is greater
than he who is in the world.

1 JOHN 4:4

Whoever therefore wants to be a friend of the world
makes himself an enemy of God.

JAMES 4:4

27

Lord, Teach My Grandchildren How to Bear Good Fruit

The kind of people we are is revealed by the kind of fruit we produce in our lives. We want our grandchildren to bear good fruit because it reveals that they are the Lord's. Jesus was raised from the dead to not only to save us so we could live with Him for all eternity, but also to live a better life now and glorify Him here on earth. The Bible says of "Him who was raised from the dead, that we should bear fruit to God" (Romans 7:4).

When Jesus was talking about bad people—false prophets—He said, "*You will know them by their fruits*" (Matthew 7:16). He explained that people must be cautious because these false prophets will "come to you in sheep's clothing, but inwardly they are ravenous wolves" (Matthew 7:15). In other words, they won't actually be what they at first appear to be.

He went on to say, "Even so, every good tree bears good fruit, but a bad tree bears bad fruit. *A good tree cannot bear bad fruit, nor can a bad tree bear good fruit*" (Matthew 7:17-18). We must judge the true nature of a person by the fruit of their life and not what they *appear* to be. Jesus said, "Therefore by their fruits you will know them" (Matthew 7:20).

Those who love God and His Word—and who invite God to live in *them* and they live in *Him*—will always bear good fruit. Those who receive Jesus have the Spirit of God living in them, and they will bear the fruit of the Spirit. "*The fruit of the Spirit is love, joy, peace, longsuffering, kindness, goodness, faithfulness, gentleness, self-control*" (Galatians 5:22-23). When you see people who have none or few of these qualities, it means they are not truly submitted to the Lord. The Holy Spirit will always produce these qualities in us if we *invite* Him and *allow* Him to do so.

Everyone needs a heart for God, His ways, and His Word. We need to pray for our grandchildren to have that heart of love for God. We don't want them to be cut down because they produced bad fruit. (See Matthew 7:19.) How many people have suffered great loss because they did what *they* wanted and did not bother to find out what *God* wanted? They reaped a crop that brought disaster to them.

Don't be afraid to ask the Holy Spirit to convict the conscience of any of your children or grandchildren if they are doing anything that will cause them to not bear good fruit in their life. Jesus said, "It is to your advantage that I go away; for *if I do not go away, the Helper will not come to you*; but if I depart, I will send Him to you. And *when He has come, He will convict the world of sin*, and of righteousness, and of judgment" (John 16:7-8). The Helper—the Holy Spirit in us—not only convicts us of sin, but He makes us able to identify the right things to do and the consequences when we don't do them.

Pray that each of Your grandchildren will have a heart that is open to the convicting power of the Holy Spirit in his or her life.

Pray also that each of your grandchildren will have a submissive heart toward God and will submit himself or herself to His will. Pray that all the confidence or self-assurance he or she has will be mixed with a servant's heart so it is used to help others and not just to promote selfish goals. Even if you did not raise your children in the ways of God, pray for them to be filled with a desire for God's Word now so they can help their children—your grandchildren—learn how to live a life that bears good fruit.

God said of His children, "They shall be My people, and I will be their God; then *I will give them one heart and one way, that they may fear Me forever, for the good of them and their children after them.* And I will make an everlasting covenant with them, that I will not turn away from doing them good; but *I will put My fear in their hearts so that they will not depart from Me*" (Jeremiah 32:38-40).

God can put reverence for Him in the hearts of our children and grandchildren. And when He does, they will not turn away from Him. Let's pray that our grandchildren will love God so much that they live a life that only produces good fruit. And that they will be known for it.

My Prayer to God

Lord, I lift up each of my grandchildren before You. (Name each grandchild before God.) Give every one of them a soft heart for You, Your Word, and Your ways. Cause them to want to know You and serve You. Keep their heart turned toward You so that no hardness of heart can settle in on them. Watch over them and keep them from turning their back on You to live in disobedience to Your ways. If that happens, give their conscience no peace until they return to You. Holy Spirit, You are the One who convicts us of sin. Convict them of any sin in their life and lead them to do the right thing.

Give each one of my grandchildren the heart of a leader and not a follower. Make them to be a follower of only You and Your ways. Grow in them a heart to know Your Word. Your Word says, "He who despises the word will be destroyed, but he who fears the commandment will be rewarded" (Proverbs 13:13). Don't let them be destroyed for lack of knowledge about Your Word. Make them to know the rewards of living by Your Word.

I know that for the one "who turns away his ear from hearing the law, even his prayer is an abomination" (Proverbs 28:9). Your Word says, "Great peace have those who love Your law, and nothing causes them to stumble" (Psalm 119:165). Give my grandchildren deep love and respect for Your laws and ways. Help them to understand how it will give them peace and keep them from falling. And pave the way for their prayers to be answered.

Jesus, You said, "Ask, and it will be given to you; seek, and you will find; knock, and it will be opened to you" (Matthew 7:7). I ask that my grandchildren will pray to You, and seek You for everything, and knock on doors that only You can open. Close doors to them that cannot be opened because they lead to the production of bad fruit. Teach them to turn to You as the source of all good fruit in their lives.

In Jesus' name I pray.

God's Word to Me

If you abide in Me, and My words abide in you,
you will ask what you desire,
and it shall be done for you. By this My Father is glorified,
that you bear much fruit; so you will be My disciples.

JOHN 15:7-8

Bear fruits worthy of repentance.

MATTHEW 3:8

The eyes of the LORD run to and fro
throughout the whole earth,
to show Himself strong on behalf of those
whose heart is loyal to Him.

2 CHRONICLES 16:9

Every tree which does not bear good fruit
is cut down and thrown into the fire.

MATTHEW 3:10

In the way of righteousness is life,
and in its pathway there is no death.

PROVERBS 12:28

28

Lord, Grow My Grandchildren's Faith to Believe That All Things Are Possible with You

*E*veryone needs a miracle at different times in his or her life. That's because we can find ourselves in impossible situations. But in order to experience a miracle, we must first have faith to believe that with God, miracles are possible.

Jesus Himself said, *"With God all things are possible"* (Matthew 19:26). He also said, *"With God nothing will be impossible"* (Luke 1:37). These verses may seem to communicate the same principle—and essentially they do—but often our mind doesn't give us the exact same reading on them. For example, we can understand that *nothing is impossible for God*, but that doesn't mean we believe God wants to do the impossible for us. We just know He *can*.

However, knowing that *with God all things are possible* means as long as we walk closely *with God*, He can do something that is impossible for us to do on our own. Or He may do something we never even thought of in order to get us out of the bad situation we're in. *We* may not be able to see a solution or a way out, but *God can* because there are *no limits* on what He can do.

We can ask God in faith to do what seems impossible in our lives, and in the lives of our grandchildren.

Our children and grandchildren need to know there is nothing God cannot do if they walk closely *with Him*—and if it is His will to do it. They must not put Him in a box and say, "God cannot solve this problem I have." They need to know they can always turn to God, believing *only He can solve their problem*...or *get them through it*...or *lift them above it*. They need faith in God and His power to do what is impossible for them to do on their own. They need faith in Jesus' words that tell them all things are possible with God.

Pray that your grandchildren will have an attitude that is not defeated or hopeless. Ask God to give them a perpetual attitude of hope and coming victory. Pray that they have faith to believe for a miracle because they know a miracle is not too hard for God. That doesn't mean we dictate to Him. Prayer is not telling God what to do. It's saying, "I believe in You, Lord, and I know You are the God of the universe and all things are possible with You. So I ask that You will do a miracle in my life today."

The opposite of faith is doubt. And doubt is a sin because God's Word says that anything that is not born of faith is a sin.

Fear comes when we doubt God's love and His will to protect us. Doubting God always makes us fearful. Having faith in God means trusting that He is the source of everything we need. Trusting Him means we know that He not only has the ability to answer our prayers, but He *wants* to do so. People who think that God is going to give up on them and walk away do not have faith. Faith in God is ongoing, unwavering, and daily, regardless of how He answers our prayers.

We must pray for our grandchildren to have strong faith in God without entertaining doubts. Even Jesus Himself did not do miracles with certain people "because of their unbelief" (Matthew 13:58). We can encourage our grandchildren that if God has not answered their prayer, it could be that He hasn't answered it *yet*. Or He is answering in a way that they do not perceive. Or He is answering in ways they are not expecting or don't understand.

Our faith is not in the power of our prayers—or in the strength of our faith. It is in God and His power working through our prayers and in response to them.

Reading God's Word grows our faith. The knowledge of how much God loves us increases our faith. The understanding of who God *is* grows our faith. Knowing God and believing in Him, and trusting His desire and ability to answer our prayers, enlarges our faith.

Let's pray that all these truths will be learned and believed by our grandchildren. In the world they are living in—now and in the future—they will need the power of God to do the impossible. Your prayers can help your grandchildren to have faith in God to do miracles that can one day save their lives.

My Prayer to God

Lord, I lift up my grandchildren to You today. (Name each grandchild before God.) Give them faith in You and Your Word that is strong enough to believe for miracles when they pray. Help them to always trust that nothing is impossible for You. Teach them that You are the God of the impossible. Help them to understand that their faith in You, their close and dependent walk with You, and Your ability to do the impossible when they pray open the door to a miraculous life.

Help my grandchildren learn to follow the leading of Your Spirit and to hear Your voice to their heart guiding them, and to not think things will just automatically work out without strong faith in You and their prayers offered to You as an act of faith. You have said in Your Word that "*if you can believe*, all things are possible to him who believes" (Mark 9:23). Enable my grandchildren to believe that *there is nothing too hard for You*, and *all things are possible* with You.

Give my grandchildren understanding that doubt is a sin because it means they don't trust You, or Your love, or Your will, or Your power to help them in any situation. Enable them to see how reading Your Word increases their faith. Jesus, You said, "If you have faith as a mustard seed," then "nothing will be impossible for you" (Matthew 17:20). Plant in each of my grandchildren a seed of faith that grows into giant faith that believes for miracles when they pray to You.

Keep my grandchildren from ever losing hope in Your ability and desire to rescue them from any hopeless situation. I pray the same for their parents and for me. I ask that You, "the God of hope," will fill my grandchildren with joy and peace in believing so they can "abound in hope by the power of the Holy Spirit" (Romans 15:13).

In Jesus' name I pray.

God's Word to Me

Ah, Lord GOD! Behold, You have made
the heavens and the earth
by Your great power and outstretched arm.
There is nothing too hard for You.

JEREMIAH 32:17

Jesus looked at them and said, "With men it is impossible,
but not with God; for with God all things are possible."

MARK 10:27

He who believes in Me, the works that I do he will do also;
and greater works than these he will do,
because I go to My Father.

JOHN 14:12

With God nothing will be impossible.

LUKE 1:37

You do not have because you do not ask.
You ask and do not receive, because you ask amiss,
that you may spend it on your pleasures.

JAMES 4:2-3

Other Books by Stormie Omartian

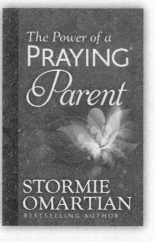

THE POWER OF PRAYING® FOR YOUR ADULT CHILDREN

Stormie says, "Our concern for our children does not stop once they step out in the world and leave home. If anything it increases. There is much more to be concerned about, but as parents we have less influence over their lives than ever. Even so, there is a way to make a big difference in their lives every day, and that is through prayer." This book by Stormie will help every parent to pray powerfully for their adult children and find peace in the process.

THE POWER OF A PRAYING® PARENT

Learn how to turn to the Lord and place every detail of your child's life in *His* hands by praying for such things as your child's safety, character development, peer pressure, friends, family relationships, and much more. Discover the joy of being part of God's work in your child's life. You don't have to be a perfect parent. You just need to be a praying parent.

PRAYER WARRIOR

Stormie says, "There is already a war going on around you, and you are in it whether you want to be or not. There is a spiritual war of good and evil—between God and His enemy—and God wants us to stand strong on His side, the side that wins. We win the war when we pray in power because prayer *is* the way we do battle." This book will help you become a powerful prayer warrior who understands the path to victory.

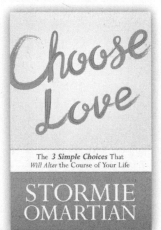

CHOOSE LOVE

We reflect God most clearly when we are motivated by the power of love in all we say and do. But first we have to understand the depth of God's love for us and receive it. Then we must learn how to effectively express our love for Him. Finally, we must learn to love others in a way that pleases Him. In these three principles we find the blessings and fulfillment God has for us.

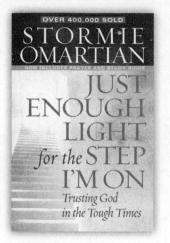

JUST ENOUGH LIGHT
FOR THE STEP I'M ON

Anyone going through changes or difficult times will appreciate Stormie's honesty, candor, and advice based on the Word of God and her experiences. This book is perfect for the pressures of today's world. She covers such topics as "Surviving Disappointment," "Walking in the Midst of the Overwhelming," "Reaching for God's Hand in Time of Loss," and "Maintaining a Passion for the Present," so you can "Move into the Future God Has for You."